MANGIAMO

MANGIAMO

Incredible Italian Dishes Inspired by
a Couple's Roots and Travels

MARK PERLIONI & ANGELA PERSICKE

Creators of Cooking with Wine

PAGE STREET
PUBLISHING CO.

Dedication

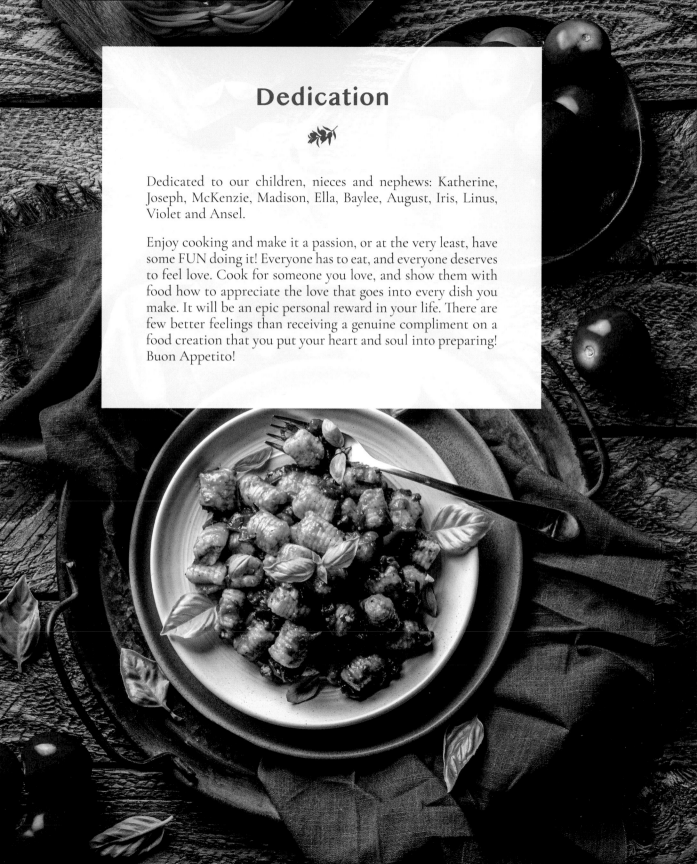

Dedicated to our children, nieces and nephews: Katherine, Joseph, McKenzie, Madison, Ella, Baylee, August, Iris, Linus, Violet and Ansel.

Enjoy cooking and make it a passion, or at the very least, have some FUN doing it! Everyone has to eat, and everyone deserves to feel love. Cook for someone you love, and show them with food how to appreciate the love that goes into every dish you make. It will be an epic personal reward in your life. There are few better feelings than receiving a genuine compliment on a food creation that you put your heart and soul into preparing! Buon Appetito!

CONTENTS

Introduction

Food is the closest thing to a common language that we have on our planet. Although extremely diverse, cuisines across the world inspire creativity, satisfy cravings and palates and bring people together. Food is passionate and emotional, an art, a craft and a science. It can even invoke fanaticism and obsession, but at the foundation it is our daily fuel for survival. We are true lovers of food and are passionate about many different cuisines, yet we still have so much to explore.

This book is, of course, based on Italian food, and that is not only because it is my heritage, but also because Angela and I absolutely love the cuisine and the Italian food culture. This passion started very young for me, seeing my Italian grandma and aunts make homemade pasta and hearing stories of my dad growing up with Italian staples like pasta e fagioli, Italian wedding soup and polenta spread across the kitchen table, along with homemade cavatelli with a delicious sauce on Sundays. Several years back, I began the process of exploring my Italian roots even further and researching the regions where my family came from, as well as the cuisine unique to those regions, to better understand some of my family's Italian dishes and traditions. My Italian family's story is like many immigrant stories, but understanding how and why we ended up in America is part of understanding the food traditions we carry on today.

My Italian Roots

Let's start with the story of my Italian grandfather. My grandfather was actually born in upstate New York in the early 1900s, making him an American citizen. His parents came to the United States temporarily right before he was born with the hopes that his future would be better if he were to be born in the land of opportunity. Like many immigrant families then and still, the "American Dream" was what they sought for my grandfather, and they faced the odds and boarded a ship, not knowing if they would make it alive or if this dream was worth the risk to them and their unborn child.

Once he was born and received that American birthright, they moved back to Celano, Italy, which is in the province of L'Aquila in the western part of the region of Abruzzo—basically, in the center of the country halfway between Rome and the Adriatic Sea to the east. He grew up there, and when he turned seventeen or eighteen, his parents sent him back to the United States to make a better life for himself as he already had citizenship. He took a ship out of Naples with his cousin, and he never returned to Italy, nor did he see his parents again.

As is the case in many Italian families that became American families, pasta was an important part of their diet. Pasta is, at its heart, a humble food with humble and inexpensive ingredients that will fill hungry bellies. In the case of my grandparents, it was the main meal at least twice a week and always on Sundays. In fact, my grandma's version of her Sunday sauce had my dad and his sisters on edge sometimes as every bit of leftover meat from the week found its way into the homemade pasta sauce on Sunday. That "tradition" didn't get carried on by my dad, and I am in no mood to revive it, either! But making homemade pasta was a staple, and I still have and use a cavatelli maker from the 1950s passed down to me through my parents.

After talking with my aunts and cousins, I find it remarkable that even in just one generation, recipes can take twists and turns and change from family to family. Some of my first cousins make "family recipes" that are so different from the recipes that I grew up eating. These recipes have the same name, have some similarities, but are absolutely different! This obviously was the result of my grandparents and their siblings cooking and baking from memory, taste and feeling rather than following any sort of written recipes. I like to think that my family's recipes live on through their evolution within each generation.

Although we have several dishes in this book that are based on recipes and traditions in my family, this is far from a cookbook of those recipes. My love for innovative food as well as imaginatively developing dishes from an existing concept is much more the theme in this book. But there are definitely some bits and pieces and a lot of the spirit of the Perlioni and DiTomasso influence from Grandpa, Grandma and the rest of my family throughout this book, as well as a few interesting family anecdotes just for fun!

My Food Story

My love for food, and specifically cooking, started when I was probably twelve or thirteen years old. I didn't invest much effort into the creation side of recipes at that age, but I did tinker a bit and enjoyed experimenting with flavors. I slowly developed a love for cooking and teaching myself how to make different things. By the time I met my wife, Angela, I was really into cooking and food. She happened to be an ultimate foodie like me, so our creativity was amplified. Our common passion drove us to do even more cooking, experimenting, recipe developing and tasting. We took food classes and food culture tours when we traveled, including ones in Italy, France and Spain. When we travel, food is a major part of the cultural experience for us and always will be. We tend to base our travel experiences on culinary adventures or food in general, and we always try to take cooking classes to explore regional dishes.

After a while, many friends and family members started requesting recipes of all the fun things we were cooking at home, and this motivated us to create a space to share our recipes. Thus our blog, Cooking with Wine, was born along with our Instagram, @cooking_with_wine. We would share photos Angela would take of the food we made as well as videos of what we were cooking on our IG stories most nights of the week, and we made our recipes accessible to everyone who visited our blog. We never imagined that this passion project would evolve into the food photography and recipe development business we have today, but we are thrilled that we are able to do something we love as a full-time job.

When Covid-19 created a need for us to move from Dallas to Houston, our blog had grown quite a bit, and Angela slowly transitioned away from her job as a professor of behavioral psychology to focus more on our business. Her focus on the photos and imagery of our creations was inspiring to me, and my passion for cooking inspired her to find more creative ways to showcase our recipes. Additionally, I had a bit more flexibility in my own career, and I decided it was time to accomplish a bucket list item: I enrolled in a formal culinary school. With years of self-training under my belt, I felt it was time to validate my skills and learn as much as I could to help our new business. My professional culinary training has brought so much more depth to our recipes and has really allowed me to understand the technique and science behind the recipes to create something not only delicious, but elevated and unforgettable.

The Inspiration Behind These Recipes

Italy is home to some of the best food inventions in the world and certainly ranks amongst the most influential and important cuisines on the planet. Although we cook a variety of foods, and we continue to explore many different cultures, Italian food and recipes are at the heart of our home cooking. We make homemade pasta at least once a week, we always have homemade pasta and pasta sauces in the freezer ready whenever the craving hits and we make many traditional Italian and Italian-inspired dishes as we continue to learn about the food culture of the different regions throughout Italy.

Although discovering my Italian roots has been the primary inspiration behind these recipes, the reality is that we are not traditionalists. We grew up in the United States and have developed our palates to appreciate a variety of flavors and cooking methods.

Some people are offended by any tweak in something that is either considered a classic or a dish from a particular area in the world, but I think of this as progression. Having attended a classical French culinary school in the United States, I experienced that adherence to tradition, and I appreciate and respect that. But I also experienced an attitude of noticing taste and technique and using them properly to elevate, change and progress dishes. Simply put, Angela and I are definitely progressive when it comes to food, but we respect traditions and foundations as well, so we will never try to say that our recipes are authentic to a specific part of the world. Everything we create is inspired by my heritage, our unique histories and my professional culinary training, as well as our travels throughout the world.

The specific recipes in this book are often inspired by classical or regional concoctions, and some are based on memories or family recipes from my childhood and my grandparents. But they are all original, sometimes quite open-minded and always something we truly love to make and eat. We are not trying to compile a bunch of classical Italian dishes, as this is not our expertise, nor is it unique. Cultures, people, life and, of course, food evolve. We enjoy being a part of the food evolution, and we hope that you keep this in mind while cooking our recipes. In fact, if you change something or tweak certain ingredients in recipes in this book, you are part of that food evolution, and we welcome it!

So here is our passion for Italian-inspired cuisine in one little collection. We want to share what we truly love with you, and the recipes in this book are our love language.

The only thing left to say is, "Let's eat," or in Italian, "Mangiamo!"

Mark Perliani   Angela Peravicke

FOR THE LOVE OF PASTA

Pasta and Rice Dishes to Enjoy Every Day of the Week and Twice on Sundays!

Several years ago, Angela and I took a trip to Italy. This was our first time exploring this beautiful country together, and that one trip has inspired many of the recipes we include in this book, especially in this chapter on pasta. Pasta recipes were not new to us by any means, and we cooked pasta together quite often. But there is something so magical about home-made pasta that we didn't quite understand until we ate our way through Italy together and experienced the nuances of each pasta shape and dish. The heart and soul that goes into making pasta from scratch really lit a culinary fire in both of us. One of the biggest takeaways from that trip, and any trip we have taken, is the importance of the use of local, quality ingredients. Wherever you live, if you start cooking with this in mind, you'll already have a head start toward success.

Since food culture is what we love, we always try to take cooking classes in other countries that we visit. While in Italy, we took one in the heart of Tuscany with Chef Francesco Calone, and it is, to this day, one of our favorite memories of any vacation. It also changed our outlook on pasta. Since that Tuscan adventure, we have probably made pasta dishes with store-bought pasta only a handful of times. The only exception for us is orzo, which we always buy from the store. In a few words, nothing compares to home-made pasta.

Sure, you can make many of the dishes in this chapter with store-bought dried pasta if you wish, but we are here to tell you that the experience will not be the same if you do. Will the pasta dishes with store-bought pasta still be delicious? Of course they will be. But they won't be magical, and our goal is to share a glimpse of magic with you that we experience when we cook these recipes at home. Many of these recipes transport us straight to a specific moment in time, often in Italy, and we feel that this is what food should be—an experience with every bite.

Potato Gnocchi

While traveling in Italy and taking cooking classes, we made egg pasta, gnocchi, ravioli and a few other memorable dishes. Since this experience, we have only made gnocchi from scratch at home and, as with homemade pasta in general, there is nothing else that can compare to the homemade version.

This base version of gnocchi is quite similar to the one we learned to make with Chef Francesco in Tuscany. It is a solid and delicious recipe that can be used as a base for many dishes, and it is our go-to recipe for homemade gnocchi.

Add your whole, unpeeled potatoes to a large pot of cold water, turn the heat to high and bring it to a boil. Once the water is boiling, turn the heat down and simmer until the potatoes are soft and offer little resistance when poked with a knife. Ensure the potatoes are covered with water the entire time, adding more if needed. This should take about 40 to 55 minutes depending on the size of the potatoes. When tender, remove the potatoes and let them cool enough to be handled.

Line a baking sheet with parchment paper and lightly dust it with flour.

Next, peel the potatoes with a paring knife and pass them through a potato ricer into a large bowl. Alternatively, you can mash them thoroughly with a fork or pass them through a tamis. You should have about 3⅓ cups (500 g) of riced cooked potato flesh after this process.

Add the flour, egg, salt and herbs, if using, to the bowl and mix these together with a serving spoon, a fork or your hands. Do not knead or overwork the dough; rather, combine until just incorporated. The dough should be quite sticky but manageable.

Turn the dough onto a clean work surface or cutting board that is lightly floured. Using just enough flour to make the dough workable, divide it into fourths and roll each section into "snakes" or ropes that are about ¾ inch (2 cm) in diameter.

Serves: 4

1⅓ lb (600 g) raw, red-skinned potatoes of similar size

1¼ cups (156 g) all-purpose flour, plus more as needed

1 large egg

2 tsp (12 g) kosher salt, plus more for boiling water

1 tbsp (2 g) finely chopped fresh herbs such as thyme, rosemary or basil (optional)

(continued)

Potato Gnocchi (Continued)

Cut each "snake" into small pillows about 1 inch (2.5 cm) long. Each piece you cut should weigh about 5 grams. If you are using a gnocchi board, gently roll each piece into a ball and, using your thumb, gently push it down into the board to make grooves. You can also use a fork for this or simply roll the gnocchi in your palms so that there are no sharp corners.

Place the gnocchi on the baking sheet in a single layer and set aside until you are ready to cook them. Make sure that the gnocchi are not touching or piled on top of each other, or they may stick.

If you prefer to make the gnocchi in advance and freeze them, as we often do, place the baking sheet of gnocchi in the freezer for about 45 minutes. Then you can remove the gnocchi to a freezer-safe bag or container without worrying about them sticking together.

To cook the gnocchi, bring a large pot of well-salted water, about 2 tablespoons (36 g) of salt per 6 to 8 quarts (6 to 8 L) of water, to a boil. Right before dropping the gnocchi into the water, give it a good stir. The swirling of the water will prevent the gnocchi from clumping together while they cook or sticking to the bottom of the pot. Allow the gnocchi to cook for 2 to 3 minutes, or until they float.

If cooking frozen gnocchi, add the gnocchi straight from the freezer to the boiling pot of water. Frozen gnocchi may need an additional minute to cook before they float.

Once all your gnocchi float, wait an additional 10 seconds and then remove them from the water with a slotted spoon, spider or strainer.

Note

One thing we want to note about the pasta and gnocchi recipes in this chapter is that homemade pasta freezes really nicely! We often make double or triple batches and freeze them so that weeknight meals are quick and easy.

Potato Thyme Gnocchi with Gorgonzola Cream Sauce and Brandied Mushrooms

This gnocchi dish was inspired by one Angela ordered in Rome. We stumbled upon this tiny restaurant as we wandered through the city. We sat outside on the sidewalk at a small table and ordered our lunch. The dish wasn't anything that would necessarily jump out at you on a menu, and there were plenty of other delicious options. It was quite simply potato gnocchi with gorgonzola cream sauce, but Angela says she can still remember the feeling she had after the first bite of the luscious and flavorful sauce with the pillow-soft gnocchi. That experience was the inspiration behind this gnocchi dish, which quickly became one of our favorites. The addition of the brandied mushrooms, which is one of our favorite original recipes, with the potato thyme gnocchi takes this dish from amazing to something you'll have to share with others.

Begin making the gnocchi according to the Potato Gnocchi recipe on page 15, including the optional thyme, and once they are ready to be boiled, set them aside. Prepare a large pot, approximately 8 quarts (8 L) or larger, of water over high heat and bring it to a boil while you prepare the sauce.

To make the gorgonzola cream sauce, add the shallot and white wine to a large skillet over medium heat and bring these to a simmer. Add the chicken stock and continue to simmer until the liquid has reduced by half. This should take approximately 10 minutes.

While the sauce reduces, make your mushrooms by heating the butter in a large skillet over medium heat. Add your mushrooms in a single layer. Do not overcrowd your pan. You can do this in batches if needed. Allow the mushrooms to cook, stirring once or twice to keep them from sticking, for 3 minutes, then toss the mushrooms and continue to cook for another 3 to 4 minutes. The mushrooms should look golden brown at this point. Reduce the heat to medium-low if they begin to brown too quickly.

(continued)

Gnocchi
1 recipe Potato Gnocchi (page 15) with thyme

Salt, for boiling water

Gorgonzola Cream Sauce
1 small (1-oz [28-g]) shallot, chopped

½ cup (118 ml) dry white wine (pinot grigio or similar)

¾ cup (177 ml) chicken stock

¾ cup (177 ml) heavy cream

¼ cup (60 g) gorgonzola cheese (see Notes)

½ tsp white wine vinegar

Kosher salt, to taste (optional)

Brandied Mushrooms
2 tbsp (28 g) unsalted butter

12 oz (340 g) oyster mushrooms, stems trimmed and cut into even pieces

2 tbsp (30 ml) brandy

⅛ tsp kosher salt

Potato Thyme Gnocchi with Gorgonzola Cream Sauce and Brandied Mushrooms (Continued)

If you cooked your mushrooms in more than one batch, return all of them to the pan at this point. Turn the heat to high for 30 seconds, then take the pan off the heat to a cold burner or to counter space. Pour your premeasured brandy into the pan and carefully light it on fire using a long matchstick or long-handled lighter (see Notes on the next page for tips). Allow the fire to burn out completely, which will take approximately 10 seconds, then return the pan to the heat over medium heat and give the mushrooms a toss. Add the salt and continue to cook for 2 to 3 more minutes. Once the mushrooms are done, you can set the pan aside and reheat them briefly in the pan before adding them to your gnocchi.

Your sauce should be properly reduced at this point. Strain the sauce through a fine sieve to a bowl to remove and discard the shallots. Add the strained sauce back into the saucepan, then add the heavy cream and gorgonzola. Reduce the heat to low and mix the sauce until the cheese melts completely, then add the white wine vinegar and stir. Taste for salt here and add a pinch, if desired.

Once your sauce and mushrooms are done, you can cook your gnocchi.

The pot of water should be boiling at this point. If not, bring it to a boil and add salt, about 2 tablespoons (36 g) per 6 to 8 quarts (6 to 8 L) of water. Right before dropping the gnocchi into the water, give it a good stir. The swirling of the water will prevent the gnocchi from clumping together while they cook or sticking to the bottom of the pot. Allow the gnocchi to cook for 2 to 3 minutes, or until they float.

Once all your gnocchi float, wait an additional 10 seconds and then remove them from the water with a slotted spoon, spider or strainer to a serving bowl.

Plate your gnocchi and spoon the sauce over the top, then top with the mushrooms and chopped parsley.

Garnish
Chopped parsley

Notes

For the gorgonzola, look for one that comes from Italy and is creamy and fragrant, yet not overly assertive.

Use extreme caution when you flambé the mushrooms. If this is your first time using this technique, you should be prepared for the fire by following these tips:

1.   Use a pan with rounded deep sides and a long handle.

2.   Remove the pan from the heat prior to adding your brandy. Your pan should be hot but not so hot that it is smoking.

3.   Always measure your brandy into a separate container and NEVER pour from the bottle.

4.   If you have a range hood vent fan, turn it on. If you don't have a range hood vent fan, move your pan to a counter space that is open and away from anything flammable.

5.   Do not lean any part of your body over the pan.

6.   Keep a lid nearby. If the fire continues to burn for longer than 15 seconds, cover the pan to put the fire out.

Potato Gnocchi with Sausage Sauce

The sausage sauce in this recipe is wonderful when paired with potato gnocchi. The sauce is so flavorful and versatile enough to use in lasagna, cannelloni, cheese ravioli or any other pasta dish. It has many applications and is also freezable, so doubling or tripling the recipe can be done on a cold Sunday! The key here is good Italian sausage, so use your favorite. This is a quick and tasty dish to make most nights of the week if you keep a batch of pre-made gnocchi and/or sausage sauce in the freezer like we often do.

Follow the instructions on page 15 to make Potato Gnocchi. The potatoes will take about 40 minutes to boil, so we recommend starting the potatoes first, then starting your sauce.

Follow the instructions on page 146 to make the Sausage Sauce. This sauce takes 45 to 60 minutes to cook. While the sauce cooks, continue making the gnocchi. Once the gnocchi are ready to be cooked, set them aside on a parchment paper–lined baking sheet.

During the final 15 minutes of cooking the sauce, you can begin heating a pot of water to cook the gnocchi.

Bring a large pot of well-salted water, about 2 tablespoons (36 g) of salt per 6 to 8 quarts (6 to 8 L) of water, to a boil. Right before dropping the gnocchi into the water, give it a good stir. The swirling of the water will prevent the gnocchi from clumping together while they cook or sticking to the bottom of the pot. Allow the gnocchi to cook for 2 to 3 minutes, or until they float.

Once all your gnocchi float, wait an additional 10 seconds and then remove them from the water with a slotted spoon, spider or strainer to a serving bowl.

Finally, taste the sauce and add salt if needed, one pinch at a time. Add the sauce and gnocchi to a serving bowl and toss to coat. Top with Parmesan, red pepper flakes and basil or your favorite garnishes.

Note
When cooking frozen gnocchi, add gnocchi straight from the freezer to the boiling pot of water. Frozen gnocchi may need an additional minute to cook before they float.

Serves: 4

Gnocchi
1 recipe Potato Gnocchi (page 15; see Note)

Salt, for boiling water

Sausage Sauce
1 recipe Sausage Sauce (page 146)

Kosher salt, to taste (optional)

Garnish
Grated Parmesan cheese

Crushed red pepper flakes

Chopped fresh basil

Sweet Potato Gnocchi

This version of gnocchi is a twist on the classic potato gnocchi recipe using sweet potatoes along with some additional flavors mixed into the dough to give it a bit more character. We find that the dough here can be quite sticky and soft, so it requires you to be a bit more delicate when shaping, but the flavor and texture we love about gnocchi really stand out with this version!

Preheat your oven to 400°F (205°C).

Wrap the sweet potato in foil and place it on a baking sheet or baking dish. Roast for 1 hour, or until a knife inserts into the flesh with little resistance. Remove it from the oven and set it aside until it is cool enough to handle.

Line a baking sheet with parchment paper and lightly dust it with flour.

Remove the sweet potato skin and puree the flesh in a food processor, mixer or blender. You should end up with about 1 cup (230 g) of puree. Next, add your sweet potato puree, salt, ricotta, pecorino cheese, 1¾ cups (219 g) of flour and nutmeg to a bowl. Mix by hand until the dough just comes together.

Turn the dough onto a clean, lightly floured work surface. Using just enough of the additional ¼ cup (31 g) flour to make the dough workable, divide the dough into fourths and roll into "snakes" about ¾ inch (2 cm) in diameter.

Cut each "snake" into small pieces about 1 inch (2.5 cm) long. Each piece you cut should weigh about 5 grams. This dough can be quite sticky and difficult to roll on the gnocchi board, so we opt for leaving the gnocchi as small pillows rather than adding indentations using the gnocchi board.

Place the gnocchi on the baking sheet in a single layer and set aside until you are ready to cook them. Make sure that the gnocchi are not touching or piled on top of each other or they may stick.

To cook the gnocchi, bring a large pot of well-salted water, about 2 tablespoons (36 g) of salt per 6 to 8 quarts (6 to 8 L) of water, to a boil. Right before dropping the gnocchi into the water, give it a good stir. The swirling of the water will prevent the gnocchi from clumping together while they cook or sticking to the bottom of the pot. Allow the gnocchi to cook for 2 to 3 minutes, or until they float. Frozen gnocchi may need an additional 1 minute to cook.

Once all your gnocchi float, wait an additional 10 seconds and then remove them from the water with a slotted spoon, spider or strainer and then serve.

Serves: 4

1 large sweet potato

1 tsp kosher salt, plus more for boiling water

½ cup (120 g) ricotta

⅛ cup (13 g) pecorino cheese

2 cups (250 g) all-purpose flour, divided

⅛ tsp ground nutmeg

Sweet Potato Gnocchi with Rosemary Garlic Brown Butter Sauce

Sweet potato gnocchi gives this dish some exciting color as well as an interesting change in taste and texture. This is a great rainy or snowy wintertime dinner that will warm your soul. The mild garlic and pungent rosemary go well with the nutty brown butter, and a good-quality white wine vinegar balances this sauce out. And when I say "sauce," it is quite simply a flavorful coating on the gnocchi and not a thick, gravy-like topping.

Follow the instructions on page 23 to make the Sweet Potato Gnocchi. The sweet potato will take about 1 hour to roast before you can use it, so plan ahead. Once your gnocchi are shaped, set aside.

To make the sauce, in a stainless or enameled cast-iron saucepan, melt the butter over medium heat and continue to cook the butter until it just starts to change color to a light brown, which will take 5 minutes or so. Once this occurs, immediately reduce the heat to low and add the rosemary, garlic and pinch of salt and stir. The butter solids will darken rather quickly, and you are only looking for a light shade of brown here, so remove the pan from the heat completely if necessary. Stir in the white wine vinegar, let it cool enough to taste for salt and add more salt, if desired. This sauce can be gently warmed to serve over the gnocchi if you wish to make it ahead of time.

Once your sauce is done, you can cook your gnocchi.

Bring a large pot of well-salted water, about 2 tablespoons (36 g) of salt per 6 to 8 quarts (6 to 8 L) of water, to a boil. Right before dropping the gnocchi into the water, give it a good stir. The swirling of the water will prevent the gnocchi from clumping together while they cook or sticking to the bottom of the pot. Allow the gnocchi to cook for 2 to 3 minutes, or until they float.

Once all your gnocchi float, wait an additional 10 seconds and then remove them from the water with a slotted spoon, spider or strainer to a serving bowl.

Plate your gnocchi, spoon the sauce over the top and garnish with chopped rosemary, Garlic Confit and shaved Pecorino Romano.

Note
To easily identify when your butter has browned, use a silver or light-colored pan so that you can see when the milk solids brown.

Serves: 4

Sweet Potato Gnocchi
1 recipe Sweet Potato Gnocchi (page 23)

Salt, for boiling water

Rosemary Garlic Brown Butter Sauce
½ cup (113 g) unsalted butter

1 tbsp (3 g) finely chopped fresh rosemary

2 cloves Garlic Confit (page 161), chopped

Pinch of kosher salt, plus more to taste

2 tsp (10 ml) white wine vinegar

Garnish
Finely chopped fresh rosemary

1–2 cloves Garlic Confit (page 161) per dish

Shaved Pecorino Romano cheese

Ricotta Gnocchi

Ricotta gnocchi is another relatively common version of gnocchi, but the ricotta provides a creamier and lighter texture. We love the herb additions of thyme, oregano and basil used here, but gnocchi are a great canvas for experimentation with different combinations of herbs and spices.

Line a baking sheet with parchment paper and lightly dust it with flour.

Mix all the ingredients together in a bowl with a fork or your hand until combined. If the dough feels a little dry, add a small amount of water by wetting your hand and continuing to knead until the dough just comes together.

Turn the dough onto a clean work surface or cutting board that is lightly floured. Using just enough additional flour to make the dough workable, about ⅓ to ⅔ cup (41 to 83 g), divide the dough into fourths and roll the sections into "snakes" or ropes that are about ½ inch (1.3 cm) in diameter.

Cut each "snake" into small pieces about ½ inch (1.3 cm) long. If you are using a gnocchi board, gently roll each piece into a ball and, using your thumb, gently push it down into the board to make grooves. You can also use a fork to create the grooves or simply cut the "snakes" and roll the gnocchi in your palms so that there are no sharp corners.

Place the gnocchi on the baking sheet in a single layer and set aside until you are ready to cook them. Make sure that the gnocchi are not touching or piled on top of each other, or they may stick.

If you prefer to make the gnocchi in advance and freeze them as we often do, place the baking sheet of gnocchi in the freezer for about 45 minutes. Then you can remove the gnocchi to a freezer-safe bag or container without worrying about them sticking together.

To cook the gnocchi, bring a large pot of well-salted water, about 2 tablespoons (36 g) of salt per 6 to 8 quarts (6 to 8 L) of water, to a boil. Right before dropping the gnocchi into the water, give it a good stir. The swirling of the water will prevent the gnocchi from clumping together while they cook or sticking to the bottom of the pot. Allow the gnocchi to cook for 2 to 3 minutes, or until they float.

If cooking frozen gnocchi, add gnocchi straight from the freezer to the boiling pot of water. Frozen gnocchi may need an additional minute to cook before they float.

Once all your gnocchi float, wait an additional 10 seconds and then remove them from the water with a slotted spoon, spider or strainer and serve.

Serves: 8

1¾ cups (454 g) ricotta, drained for 30 minutes in a colander (see Note)

2 large eggs

1¼ cups (125 g) grated Parmesan cheese

1 cup (125 g) all-purpose flour, plus more as needed

1 tsp kosher salt

¼ tsp black pepper

¼ tsp minced fresh thyme

¼ tsp minced fresh oregano

½ tsp minced fresh basil

Note

If making ricotta gnocchi using store-bought ricotta, you will likely need to add about ⅓ to ½ cup (41 to 63 g) more flour even after straining the ricotta because the store-bought versions often have more moisture. Every ricotta brand is different, so add just enough flour for the dough to be manageable.

Ricotta Gnocchi Primavera

Primavera simply means "spring" in Italian, but in many restaurants in the United States, it is used to describe pasta made with vegetables. Using fresh, seasonal quality vegetables in this dish is paramount to highlight all the bright flavors of the season. This is our version, and using a wide array of these fresh seasonal vegetables, as well as the light and fluffy ricotta gnocchi, has quickly made this one of our favorites to enjoy on the back porch when the weather is nice!

Begin by making the Ricotta Gnocchi according to the directions on page 27 and set aside while you prepare the sauce and vegetables.

Bring a large pot of water to a boil. Prepare a large bowl of ice water and set it nearby. Add the asparagus tips to the boiling water for 1½ minutes. Remove them to the ice water to shock them, then allow them to drain on a towel.

Next, cut the stems of the broccolini into 1-inch (2.5-cm)-long segments and set them aside from the broccolini heads. Blanch these in separate batches. Cook the stems for 2 to 3 minutes and the heads for 1 minute. Remove each batch to the ice water and drain on a towel. Set these aside with the asparagus tips.

To make the sauce, add the olive oil to a large pan over medium-low heat. Next, add the diced shallots and "sweat" them for 2 to 3 minutes, until translucent without browning. Add the garlic, cook for a minute until fragrant and then add the wine. Continue to cook gently over medium-low to medium heat for 5 minutes, reducing the wine to about 1 to 2 tablespoons (15 to 30 ml).

Once the wine has reduced, increase the heat to medium, add the tomatoes and cook for 1 minute, then add the peppers and cook for another minute. Next add 1 teaspoon of basil, ½ teaspoon of thyme, ½ teaspoon of oregano and 1 teaspoon of salt. Cook this mixture for 10 minutes, stirring occasionally.

(continued)

Serves: 8

1 recipe Ricotta Gnocchi (page 27)

¾ cup (100 g) asparagus tips

2–3 oz (57–85 g) broccolini

2 tbsp (30 ml) olive oil

1 large (2-oz [57-g]) shallot, finely diced

4–5 cloves garlic, minced

⅔ cup (158 ml) dry white wine (pinot grigio or sauvignon blanc are good options)

2½ cups (500 g) peeled, seeded and diced tomatoes

½ cup (70 g) thinly sliced red and/or yellow bell peppers

2 tbsp plus 1 tsp (8 g) finely chopped fresh basil, divided

1½ tsp (1 g) finely chopped fresh thyme, divided

1½ tsp (1 g) finely chopped fresh oregano, divided

1½ tsp (9 g) kosher salt, divided, plus more for boiling water

Ricotta Gnocchi Primavera (Continued)

After 10 minutes, add the zucchini, asparagus and broccolini and stir. Add the remaining 2 tablespoons (6 g) of basil, 1 teaspoon of thyme and 1 teaspoon of oregano. Turn the heat to low, stir and add the last ½ teaspoon of kosher salt. Simmer on low for another 10 to 12 minutes. This mixture may seem dry as you simmer it, but don't worry because you will be adding between ½ to 1 cup (118 to 237 ml) of pasta water from the gnocchi to finish the sauce and achieve the desired sauce consistency.

While the sauce simmers, bring a large pot of well-salted water, about 2 tablespoons (36 g) of salt per 6 to 8 quarts (6 to 8 L) of water, to a boil. Right before dropping the gnocchi into the water, give it a good stir. The swirling of the water will prevent the gnocchi from clumping together while they cook or sticking to the bottom of the pot. Allow the gnocchi to cook for 2 to 3 minutes, or until they float.

Once all your gnocchi float, wait an additional 10 seconds and then remove them from the water with a slotted spoon, spider or strainer, into a serving bowl.

Add ½ cup (118 ml) of pasta water to the sauce and stir to incorporate. If your sauce still appears too dry, add an additional ¼ to ½ cup (59 to 118 ml) as needed. The sauce should not be soupy but should have enough liquid to coat the gnocchi.

Once the sauce has reached the desired consistency, transfer it to the serving bowl with the gnocchi and toss to combine. Garnish with shaved Parmesan, fresh basil and crushed red pepper flakes.

½ cup (70 g) medium-diced zucchini

Garnish
Shaved Parmesan

Fresh basil

Crushed red pepper flakes

Ricotta Gnocchi with Fresh Tomato Sauce

This is a fairly simple way to enjoy the ricotta gnocchi, particularly when tomatoes are in season at the height of summer. We also enjoy this throughout the year when we want something fresh and vibrant for dinner. The fresh tomato sauce is quick and easy to make, and the whole recipe can be ready in under an hour, especially if you take our advice and freeze some of the ricotta gnocchi every time you make a full batch.

Make a half recipe of Ricotta Gnocchi according to the directions on page 27, and once the gnocchi are ready to be boiled, set them aside while you prepare the sauce.

Next, make the fresh tomato sauce. Chop the tomatoes and remove and discard the seeds. You will end up with approximately 1½ pounds (680 g) of chopped tomatoes to use in the sauce. Add the Garlic-Infused Olive Oil to a large skillet over medium heat, then add the onion and stir to coat in oil. Cook for 5 minutes, stirring occasionally, until translucent but not brown. Next, add the tomato paste and stir to combine. Cook for 1 minute, stirring constantly. After 1 to 2 minutes, add the tomatoes. Increase the heat to medium-high and cook uncovered, stirring occasionally for 5 minutes, then add the white wine and stir. Continue cooking the sauce for another 3 minutes, then reduce the heat to medium, add the basil and stir. Cook for 1 to 2 more minutes, then remove from the heat and stir in the salt, pepper and balsamic.

While the sauce cooks, bring a large pot of well-salted water, about 2 tablespoons (36 g) of salt per 6 to 8 quarts (6 to 8 L) of water, to a boil. Right before dropping the gnocchi into the water, give it a good stir. The swirling of the water will prevent the gnocchi from clumping together while they cook or sticking to the bottom of the pot. Allow the gnocchi to cook for 2 to 3 minutes, or until they float.

Once all your gnocchi float, wait an additional 10 seconds and then remove them from the water with a slotted spoon, spider or strainer into a serving bowl.

When the sauce is ready, transfer it to the serving bowl with the gnocchi and toss to combine, then serve with freshly grated Parmesan cheese, fresh basil and crushed red pepper flakes.

Note
If you don't have or want to make Garlic-Infused Olive Oil, simply replace this with the same amount of regular olive oil, then add 1 clove of minced garlic at the same time as the tomato paste.

Serves: 4

Ricotta Gnocchi
½ recipe Ricotta Gnocchi (page 27)

Salt, for boiling water

Fresh Tomato Sauce
2 lb (907 g) tomatoes (Campari or your choice)

3 tbsp (44 ml) Garlic-Infused Olive Oil (page 161; see Note)

1 medium (4-oz [113-g]) onion, small dice

2 tbsp (28 g) tomato paste

½ cup (118 ml) dry white wine

¼ cup (10 g) chopped fresh basil

2 tsp (12 g) kosher salt

¼ tsp pepper

1 tsp balsamic vinegar

Garnish
Freshly grated Parmesan cheese

Fresh basil

Crushed red pepper flakes

Eggless Pasta Dough

This is the most basic of pasta doughs and, honestly, my personal preference over egg pasta for many applications. This version can use Tipo 00 flour, made from soft wheat, or semolina flour, made from hard wheat, and they each provide a different mouthfeel and taste that should be experienced. A variety of pasta shapes can be made with this eggless pasta dough, but we only included directions for shaping cavatelli since this pasta shape is what I grew up eating, and it is near and dear to my heart.

A note here: "Americanization" of labels for flours and the milling process can be confusing, especially when comparing them with Italian flours. Semolina and semola flour are both names that you may see on products from hard wheat flour. For best results, finely ground flour is what you should look for, but it could be labeled with either of these names in US grocery stores. If it is Italian flour it will have "rimacinata" on the package, and that is what you want. If a coarse grind of semolina is all you can find, it's not the end of the world! We've tried this recipe with the coarser grind and it is perfectly fine.

Place the flour on a clean work surface and make a well in the middle of the flour. Add the oil, water and salt and incorporate with a fork until you can work it with your hands.

Knead the dough, using the heel of your hand to push down into the flat surface of the table, then folding the dough onto itself and then rotating the dough. Repeat this until the dough forms a smooth ball and bounces back a little when pressed into with your finger. If your dough is dry, you can add water by the teaspoon until it becomes silky and smooth. This is especially true when using the semolina version of this recipe. This kneading process will take about 10 minutes.

Make a fat disc about 2 inches (5 cm) thick, then wrap it in plastic wrap and rest at room temperature for at least 15 minutes and up to 2 hours. Once it has rested, your dough is ready to shape and use.

(continued)

Serves: 4

If Using Tipo 00 Flour Dough

3 cups (400 g) Tipo 00 flour

1½ tbsp (22 ml) olive oil

⅔ cup (158 ml) water

1 tsp kosher salt, plus more for boiling water

If Using Semolina Dough

3 cups (400 g) semola or semolina flour

1½ tbsp (22 ml) olive oil

¾ cup (177 ml) water

1 tsp kosher salt, plus more for boiling water

Eggless Pasta Dough (Continued)

To shape the pasta as cavatelli, remove the plastic wrap from the dough and divide the dough into eight pieces. Roll each piece into a thin snake or rope smaller than your pinkie finger in diameter, about ¼ inch (6 mm). Using a knife, cut the rope into 1-inch (2.5-cm) segments. Next, with three fingers or a butter knife, press down into each segment and pull or drag it towards you. This will create an indentation in the segment and the edges will slightly curl in for that typical cavatelli shape. If you aren't familiar with cavatelli, each noodle should resemble a hot dog bun or sea shell. Alternatively, you can use the gnocchi board and a bench scraper or knife to create the same shape but with grooves, as shown in the photo. We prefer to have the grooves to catch more sauce, but you can use whatever you have available to make these.

Once you finish shaping your pasta, you can use it immediately or spread it out on a baking sheet or table to dry for 4 hours or longer, up to 3 days in humid climates. Once dried completely, you can place the dough in an airtight container and store it in your pantry. Because this pasta does not contain fresh ingredients like eggs or milk, you do not need to store it in the freezer or refrigerator, and you can use it just like you would any store-bought dried pasta.

To cook the pasta, bring a large pot of well-salted water, about 2 tablespoons (36 g) of salt per 6 to 8 quarts (6 to 8 L) of water, to a boil.

If cooking the eggless pasta on the same day that it was made, once boiling, add your pasta and allow it to cook for approximately 5 minutes. If cooking dried eggless pasta, cook it for 7 to 10 minutes.

Take one noodle out and test it for doneness. When your pasta is done, it should be al dente, meaning it will have a bite, but should not taste like raw flour.

Remove your pasta to a colander to drain briefly, then add it to a serving bowl with your desired sauce.

Cavatelli with Lamb Ragù

Since cavatelli reminds me of some of my favorite pasta dishes as a kid and memories of making homemade cavatelli with Grandma, I wanted to make a special sauce for it. And what better protein to pay homage to Abruzzo than lamb?

When I was young, we made cavatelli using a hand-crank machine and, inevitably, one of the rounded and misshapen ends would wind up in the pot. Whoever got that piece of pasta on their plate believed it was good luck while the rest of the family would claim the opposite! Although we now make cavatelli by hand, from time to time we will bring out the old cavatelli machine, and we stick to the "good luck" version of this story for our own family member who winds up with the misshapen end on their dinner plate. Everybody deserves a bit of good luck!

I have served this dish to multiple people where the inevitable person who "isn't a fan of lamb" is present. Angela used to be one of these people until I opened her mind to a world of delicious lamb dishes. I'm just going to say it: if you aren't a fan of lamb, at worst you will like this ragù and at best you will be a lamb convert! This is now one of Angela's favorite sauces.

First, cut the lamb into large bite-sized cubes and place them in a large bowl. Add the salt and pepper to the lamb, and combine.

Add the oil to a large skillet over high heat and sear the lamb in batches to achieve some browning. You are not trying to cook the lamb here, so no need to cook it for longer than it takes to get some color on all sides of each cube. This will take about 3 minutes per batch. Set the browned lamb aside.

In the same pan that you used to brown the lamb, turn the heat down to medium and add the tomato paste. Stir constantly for about 30 seconds, then add the celery, carrots and onion and cook for 5 to 7 minutes, or until the onion is translucent and begins to get some color. Add the garlic and stir for 15 seconds. Then add the wine and scrape the bottom of the pan to deglaze it.

Next, add the lamb back to the pan and cook over medium heat for 5 minutes. Add the beef stock, balsamic vinegar, rosemary, parsley, thyme, oregano, bay leaves and fennel seeds. Stir to combine and bring to a boil. Reduce the heat to low, cover and simmer for 1½ to 2 hours, stirring and scraping the bottom occasionally.

(continued)

Serves: 4

Lamb Ragù

1 lb 5 oz (600 g) lamb shoulder, deboned and trimmed

1 tbsp (18 g) kosher salt, plus more to taste

½ tsp black pepper

2 tbsp (30 ml) vegetable oil

2 tbsp (28 g) tomato paste

2 (1-oz [28-g]) ribs celery, chopped

2 medium (3-oz [85-g]) carrots, chopped

1 medium (6-oz [170-g]) onion, chopped

1 tbsp (10 g) minced garlic

1 cup (237 ml) dry red wine

1 cup (237 ml) beef stock

1 tsp balsamic vinegar

2 tsp (2 g) chopped fresh rosemary

2 tsp (2 g) chopped fresh parsley

2 tsp (2 g) chopped fresh thyme

2 tsp (2 g) chopped fresh oregano

2 bay leaves

1 tsp whole fennel seeds, lightly toasted in a dry pan for 1 minute

¼ cup (59 ml) heavy cream

Cavatelli with Lamb Ragù (Continued)

While the ragù cooks, make the Eggless Pasta Dough on page 35 and shape it into cavatelli. Set the cavatelli aside on a large baking sheet.

When your ragù is almost ready, bring a large pot of well-salted water, about 2 tablespoons (36 g) of salt per 6 to 8 quarts (6 to 8 L) of water, to a boil. Once boiling, add the cavatelli and allow them to cook for 5 minutes. Take one cavatelli out and test it for doneness. When done, they should be al dente, meaning they will have a bite, but should not taste like raw flour.

Remove to a colander to drain briefly, then add to a serving bowl.

Once the cavatelli are done, add the cream to the ragù, stir and cook for just a few minutes. Remove the bay leaves and add additional salt to taste.

Serve the ragù over the cavatelli and garnish with freshly grated Parmesan cheese, crushed red pepper flakes and fresh basil.

Cavatelli
1 recipe Eggless Pasta Dough (page 35), shaped into cavatelli

Salt, for boiling water

Garnish
Grated Parmesan cheese

Crushed red pepper flakes

Fresh basil leaves

Cavatelli with Roasted Red Pepper Pesto Sauce, Basil Cream and Burrata

Here is another great addition to cavatelli that is full of bright and rich flavors. Fresh, roasted red peppers and burrata are an excellent pairing and take this humble pasta to classy heights. Crushed red pepper flakes, which were my grandpa's secret weapon in food flavoring, should top it off if you like a bit of spicy heat to go with the decadent burrata.

Follow the directions on page 35 to make Eggless Pasta Dough. While the pasta dough rests, make the Roasted Red Pepper Pesto (page 150), then shape the dough into cavatelli following the instructions on page 36.

Next, follow the directions on page 157 to make the Basil Cream Sauce and set it aside in the fridge.

For this dish, we make the pesto in a blender for a smooth creamy texture. Add the pesto sauce to a medium pan and gently warm it over low heat while the cavatelli cook.

To cook the cavatelli, bring a large pot of well-salted water, about 2 tablespoons (36 g) of salt per 6 to 8 quarts (6 to 8 L) of water, to a boil. Once boiling, add the cavatelli and allow them to cook for 5 minutes. Take one cavatelli out and test it for doneness. They should be al dente, meaning they will have a bite, but should not taste like raw flour.

Remove the cavatelli from the water using a slotted spoon or spider and place them directly into the saucepan with the pesto sauce. Stir to coat completely, then serve topped with half of a burrata ball per plate, a drizzle of olive oil, the Basil Cream Sauce, fresh basil, crushed red pepper flakes and cracked black pepper.

Serves: 4

Cavatelli
1 recipe Eggless Pasta Dough (page 35), shaped into cavatelli

Roasted Red Pepper Pesto Sauce
½ recipe (about ¾ cups [177 g]) Red Pepper Pesto (page 150)

Toppings
Drizzle of Basil Cream Sauce (page 157)

2 (4-oz [113-g]) burrata balls

High-quality extra virgin olive oil

Fresh basil

Crushed red pepper flakes

Cracked black pepper

Multipurpose Pasta Dough

Many traditional pasta doughs include olive oil, but we prefer the softness of butter in this one. And, of course, many egg pasta doughs could include twice as many egg yolks or more. We have tried it, and the silky texture added can be somewhat compromised by the "egginess" in taste in our opinion. Our version is not the most traditional pasta dough, but when cooked in liberally salted water, it yields an amazing texture and taste that will have you hooked. So here you have it, our go-to everyday pasta dough that we make and eat at least once a week!

Pile the flour on a clean flat surface. In the center of the pile, make a well with your fingers all the way to the bottom, leaving a wall of flour as a barrier around the outside. Next, add the butter, milk, egg and egg yolks to the center of the well.

With a fork, beat the egg mixture and slowly incorporate the flour from the outside edges. Use a bench scraper to assist this process by moving the flour into the center. Once the egg mixture begins to form a sticky mass and is no longer runny, use your bench scraper to fold the remaining flour into the dough until you are able to bring the dough together by hand. It will be very sticky at this point.

Knead the dough, using the heel of your hand to push down into the flat surface of the table, then folding the dough onto itself and then rotating the dough. Repeat this until the dough forms a smooth ball. This should take about 5 to 10 minutes.

At this point, your dough should not look dry and flaky. On the other hand, it should not be sticky either, so you may need to adjust with water or flour until you achieve a smooth, almost leather-like feeling. If you notice the dough looks dry, wet the tips of one or two fingers and continue to knead. Repeat this as needed. If your dough appears too wet, add a pinch of flour at a time, knead, and repeat as necessary.

Once the dough is ready, press the dough into a disc approximately 2 inches (5 cm) thick and wrap it in plastic wrap. Place it in the fridge for at least 30 minutes and up to 24 hours to rest.

(continued)

Serves: 4

1½ cups (200 g) Tipo 00 flour, plus more as needed

2 tsp (10 ml) melted unsalted butter

2 tsp (10 ml) whole milk

1 large whole egg

3 large egg yolks

Multipurpose Pasta Dough (Continued)

After resting your dough, remove it from the refrigerator and let it sit at room temperature for 10 minutes inside the plastic wrap. Unwrap and knead it on a lightly floured surface for a few minutes by hand.

Cut the dough into manageable pieces about the size of the palm of your hand, approximately 3 to 3½ ounces (85 to 100 g) per piece. Press each piece on a flat surface with your hands to flatten it to about ¼ inch (6 mm) thick. Run each piece through a pasta roller starting with the widest setting.

Fold and run through on the widest setting a total of three times. If it gets too wide you can fold the sides in to make it thinner. If it rips or tears, simply fold it over and start again. Run it through the next lowest setting two more times, folding in between.

Then run the sheet through once at the next lowest setting and continue until your desired thickness is achieved. We leave it slightly thicker for spaghetti and fettuccine, and thinner for lasagna, cannelloni, pappardelle and ravioli. Every roller is different, so you may need to try out a few thicknesses to find what you prefer.

Lay your pasta sheet on a flat surface dusted with flour while you roll out the rest of the dough.

Alternatively, you can roll the pasta dough out with a rolling pin, but be prepared to really put some muscle into it. You want to roll the sheet out until you can see the light through it when you hold it up.

Cut your pasta sheets as desired for the dish. Sprinkle and toss with semolina flour to prevent the pasta from sticking together. Use or freeze immediately.

To cook your pasta, bring a large pot of well-salted water, about 2 tablespoons (36 g) of salt per 6 to 8 quarts (6 to 8 L) of water, to a boil. Once boiling, add the pasta and allow it to cook for 2 to 3 minutes. Take one noodle out and test it for doneness. The pasta should be al dente, meaning it will have a bite, but should be cooked and not have a raw flour taste. If cooking frozen pasta, add 1 additional minute to your cook time.

Spaghetti and Meatballs

This was one of three weekly meals for my dad and his siblings growing up, and it was usually served on Sunday and/or Thursday. Traditionally in Italy, meatballs are not served on top of pasta like what is commonly seen here in the United States, so the tradition of eating spaghetti with meatballs once or twice a week likely started with my grandma's influence growing up in America. Although, it may not have always been spaghetti as the pasta served. It could very well have been cavatelli, fettuccine or whatever pasta Grandma had made that week, but it was given the beloved name "spaghetti and meatballs." I grew up eating a version of this as well, although store-bought pasta sometimes took the place of the homemade versions Grandma made.

We've revived the homemade tradition with this recipe and updated the recipe to reflect our tastes with the most flavorful homemade meatballs and our version of Grandma's Sunday Sauce. Also, we recommend using Wagyu ground beef if you can find it to make the meatballs extra tender and flavorful.

Follow the instructions on page 42 to make the Multipurpose Pasta Dough. For spaghetti, take your pasta sheets and cut them into strips approximately ⅛ inch (3 mm) wide. Set the pasta aside until you are ready to cook it.

Follow the instructions to make Grandma's Sunday Sauce (page 145), or if you made this sauce in advance and/or froze it, warm 2 to 3 cups (473 to 710 ml) of the sauce in a large pot over low heat.

To make the meatballs, preheat the oven to 375°F (190°C) and line a large baking dish with parchment paper. In a bowl, mix all of the meatball ingredients together to thoroughly combine. Roll this mixture into balls about 1⅕ to 1¼ inches (3 to 4 cm) in diameter, depending on your size preference. Place the formed meatballs on the baking dish and bake in the preheated oven for 30 minutes, or until the meatballs are a light chocolate brown. Let the meatballs cool down for 10 to 15 minutes, then add them to the sauce and turn to coat.

(continued)

Serves: 4

Pasta
1 recipe Multipurpose Pasta Dough (page 42) for spaghetti

Salt, for boiling water

Sauce
2–3 cups (473–710 ml) Grandma's Sunday Sauce (about ¼ recipe; page 145; see Notes)

Meatballs
¾ lb (340 g) ground beef (chuck or 80/20)

¼ lb (113 g) ground pork

2 cloves Garlic Confit (page 161), finely chopped

2 tsp (4 g) crushed red pepper

1 tsp kosher salt

½ tsp black pepper

2 tsp (2 g) chopped fresh parsley

2 tsp (2 g) chopped fresh oregano

2 tsp (2 g) chopped fresh basil

2 tsp (4 g) onion powder

1 egg yolk

¼ cup (25 g) panko bread crumbs, toasted lightly in a dry pan

Spaghetti and Meatballs (Continued)

Bring a large pot of well-salted water, about 2 tablespoons (36 g) of salt per 6 to 8 quarts (6 to 8 L) of water, to a boil. Once boiling, add the pasta and allow it to cook for 2 to 3 minutes. Take one noodle out and test it for doneness. The pasta should be al dente, meaning it will have a bite, but should be cooked and not have a raw flour taste.

Toss the cooked spaghetti in a large bowl with just enough sauce to coat the noodles. Serve the remaining sauce in a bowl at the table along with the garnishes, so that each individual can add more sauce and garnishes per their preferences.

Notes

Grandma's Sunday Sauce from start to finish takes about 2 hours, so we recommend making the sauce in advance, freezing it in portions and reheating a portion of the sauce in a saucepan on the stove if you want to make this recipe during the week when you don't have time for a 2-hour sauce.

Alternatively, if you do not have time to make the sauce and really want to enjoy this recipe, you can make the meatballs with the Quick Tomato Sauce (page 114) recipe instead.

Garnish

Freshly grated Parmesan cheese

Crushed red pepper flakes

High-quality extra virgin olive oil

Thinly sliced basil leaves

Parmesan-Crusted Shrimp Fra Diavolo Spaghetti

Shrimp and pasta is such a satisfying dish to us. It always looks amazing, it has multiple textures and the taste is out of this world. A little spiciness makes this recipe our version of "fra diavolo," and the spices in this dish complement shrimp nicely. The fresh sauce is packed with flavor and doesn't need to be used exclusively in this dish, so experiment! Additionally, the shrimp can be made as a stand-alone dish or appetizer, but we love it all together.

Follow the instructions on page 42 to make the Multipurpose Pasta Dough. For spaghetti, take your pasta sheets and cut them into strips approximately ⅛ inch (3 mm) wide. Once cut, set the spaghetti aside while you make the shrimp and sauce.

Combine the shrimp with all of the Shrimp Marinade ingredients in a bowl or sealable plastic bag and place it in the refrigerator for 15 to 20 minutes.

Meanwhile, for the shrimp fry, set up a breading station near your stovetop. Put the flour on one plate, mix the eggs and water in a small bowl and mix the Parmesan and bread crumbs on a third plate. Heat the oil in the pan over medium heat for about 3 minutes. After 3 minutes of heating, test the oil by sprinkling in a few bread crumbs. If the oil sizzles and bubbles, and doesn't immediately turn the bread crumbs brown, then you are ready to fry the shrimp. If you have a thermometer, you are looking for 350°F (177°C).

Remove the shrimp from the marinade and reserve the marinade to start the sauce. Holding the tail of the shrimp, dredge it in flour and gently shake off any excess. Immediately coat it in the egg followed by the bread crumb and Parmesan mixture. You can coat four or five and then fry them in batches to a golden-brown color. Fry each side of the shrimp for 1 to 1½ minutes. Adjust the heat as necessary if the shrimp browns too quickly or if they take longer than about a minute a side to become golden brown. Remove the shrimp to an oven-safe plate or a baking sheet and repeat the process until all of the shrimp are done. Set aside.

(continued)

Serves: 4

Pasta

1 recipe Multipurpose Pasta Dough (page 42) for spaghetti

Salt, for boiling water

Shrimp Marinade

1 lb (454 g) shrimp, peeled and deveined, tails on (about 16 large/extra-large shrimp work well)

3 tbsp (44 ml) olive oil

2 tsp (4 g) crushed red pepper flakes

1 tsp kosher salt

½ tsp black pepper

Shrimp Fry

1 cup (125 g) all-purpose flour

2 large eggs

1 tbsp (15 ml) water

¼ cup (25 g) freshly grated Parmesan cheese

¼ cup (25 g) panko bread crumbs

1 cup (240 ml) neutral cooking oil, like grapeseed, canola or vegetable (see Notes)

Parmesan-Crusted Shrimp Fra Diavolo Spaghetti (Continued)

Start your sauce by adding the marinade to a large pan over medium to medium-low heat. Add the onion and chile pepper and sauté gently for 4 to 5 minutes, until the onion is translucent but not brown. Add the minced garlic, continue to cook for about a minute, and then add the wine and turn the heat up to medium. Cook until the wine is reduced by about 70 percent to less than ¼ cup (59 ml) and you cannot smell the alcohol any longer. This will take 4 to 5 minutes, but be patient and don't turn the heat up above medium.

Add the tomatoes, pepper, oregano and basil and cook over medium heat for 5 to 8 minutes, stirring occasionally, until the tomatoes break down and create a chunky sauce.

While you wait for the sauce to finish, preheat your oven to 200°F (93°C) and bring a large pot of well-salted water, about 2 tablespoons (36 g) of salt per 6 to 8 quarts (6 to 8 L) of water, to a boil for the pasta.

To finish the sauce, add the vinegar, parsley and lemon zest, stir and re-season with salt, if necessary. When your sauce is ready, place your shrimp in the oven to keep warm.

Once the pot of water is boiling, add the pasta and allow it to cook for 2 to 3 minutes. Take one noodle out and test it for doneness. The pasta should be al dente, meaning it will have a bite, but should not taste like raw flour.

Once the pasta is done, transfer it directly to the pan with the sauce and toss it all together to coat. Remove your pasta to a serving bowl and place the warmed shrimp on top. Garnish with fresh basil, Parmesan and crushed red pepper flakes.

Sauce

⅔ cup (100 g) diced onion

1 Fresno chile pepper, finely chopped (see Notes)

3 cloves garlic, minced

¾ cup (177 ml) dry white wine

4 cups (750 g) peeled, seeded and chopped tomatoes

½ tsp cracked black pepper

2 tbsp (6 g) chopped fresh oregano

2 tbsp (6 g) chopped fresh basil

½ tsp white wine vinegar

1 tbsp (4 g) chopped fresh parsley

1 tsp finely grated lemon zest

Salt, to taste

Garnish

Chopped fresh basil

Freshly grated Parmesan cheese

Crushed red pepper flakes

Notes

For shallow frying the shrimp, you may need more or less oil depending on the size of your pan—ours is a 10-inch (25-cm) sauté pan—but you are only looking for the oil to be ¼ to ⅓ inch (6 to 8 mm) deep in the pan.

You can substitute another chile pepper for the Fresno chile pepper. Fresno peppers can be slightly spicier than jalapeños but have a fruitier flavor.

Seared Scallop Pappardelle with Lavender Vanilla Vodka Cream Sauce

Typically, you will find vodka sauces made with tomatoes, but this version omits the tomatoes and adds several other unique ingredients that pair perfectly with scallops. We spent a good amount of time creating this dish with the combination of flavors you see here. It was well worth the effort, and this is probably one of the recipes in this book that we are most proud of. I always encourage tasting things along the cooking process where possible, but in the case of this cream sauce, it's a little bit different. It simply doesn't taste very good during the cooking process until the end stages, primarily because the vodka needs to cook down and out, and there is an awful lot of ingredient-melding going on. So, we ask you to have some faith in the process, because at the end it transforms into liquid happiness!

Follow the instructions on page 42 to make the Multipurpose Pasta Dough. While the pasta dough is resting, prepare your scallops.

Ensure that the abductor muscle is removed from each scallop. It is the small bulging piece of meat on the side of each scallop, unless they were cleaned prior to purchasing. Dry the scallops well using a paper towel and place them on a rack to air dry in the refrigerator for about an hour.

While your scallops chill in the refrigerator, roll and cut your pappardelle. Take your pasta sheets and cut them into strips approximately 1 inch (2.5 cm) wide. Set them aside until your sauce is complete.

Next start the sauce by adding the vodka, fish stock, vanilla, lavender, lemon zest, lemon thyme, ½ teaspoon of salt and pepper to a saucepan. Stir to combine and reduce over medium heat by a third. This should take about 20 minutes or so. Once reduced, strain out the solids using a fine sieve and return the strained liquid to the saucepan.

Add the cream and 1 tablespoon (15 ml) of lemon juice and simmer to reduce to a thickened sauce consistency. This will take about 40 minutes, so be patient and allow the sauce to do its thing. Resist the urge to speed up the process in any way here.

(continued)

Serves: 4

Pappardelle

1 recipe Multipurpose Pasta Dough (page 42) for pappardelle

Salt, for boiling water

Scallops

12–16 large sea scallops (3–4 per person depending on how large they are)

2 tsp (12 g) kosher salt

1 tsp fine ground white pepper

1 tbsp (14 g) unsalted butter

Lavender Vanilla Vodka Cream Sauce

¼ cup (59 ml) vodka

1 cup (237 ml) fish stock

½ tsp vanilla extract

¼ tsp food-grade dried lavender

1 tsp lemon zest, plus more to garnish

1 sprig lemon thyme, lemon basil or thyme, plus more to garnish

1 tsp kosher salt, divided

¼ tsp white pepper

1¾ cups (414 ml) heavy cream

1 tbsp plus 2 tsp (25 ml) lemon juice, divided

Seared Scallop Pappardelle with Lavender Vanilla Vodka Cream Sauce (Continued)

About 10 minutes before the sauce is done, bring a large pot of well-salted water, about 2 tablespoons (36 g) of salt per 6 to 8 quarts (6 to 8 L) of water, to a boil.

Once the sauce is done, it should be a pourable but thick sauce that will stick to the pasta. Add the final 2 teaspoons (10 ml) of lemon juice and ½ teaspoon of kosher salt and taste for seasoning.

When the sauce is done, add your pasta to the boiling water. Allow the pasta to cook for 2 to 3 minutes. Take one noodle out and test it for doneness. The pasta should be al dente, meaning it will have a bite, but should not taste like raw flour. Remove it to a colander, and drizzle with a small amount of olive oil and toss to prevent the pasta from sticking.

To sear the scallops, heat a large nonstick or cast-iron skillet over medium-high heat. Remove your scallops from the fridge and season with salt and pepper on both sides. Add the butter to the pan, just enough to barely coat the pan. As soon as the butter melts, quickly place your scallops in the pan. They will need about 1½ to 2 minutes per side, or until there is some caramelization forming. If you are cooking in batches, wipe the pan dry and add fresh butter with each batch.

To serve, add the pasta to a large bowl with enough sauce to coat the pappardelle. Plate the pasta and top with the scallops. Drizzle a bit more sauce over the top and garnish with a small amount of lemon zest and lemon thyme.

Note
Make absolutely sure you aren't crowding the pan when you sear the scallops. You are better off doing them in two or even three batches if you need to. Too many scallops and you'll just end up steaming them without any caramelization.

Fettuccine with White Wine Clam Sauce

Pasta, typically linguine, with white wine clam sauce is a well-known and beloved dish that can be found on many Italian restaurant menus here in the United States. When I was a kid, we didn't eat out too often, but if we ever went to an Italian restaurant, pasta with a white wine clam sauce was my favorite thing to order. This isn't the most common food that a child would generally eat, but I could never get enough of that taste from the white wine and clam juice, and I certainly sopped it all up with some nice Italian bread. I still love this dish, and once I started cooking on my own, this was one of the dishes I had to perfect. Our version is an absolute flavor bomb, something I never experienced at any restaurant. Making the flavors in the sauce sing along with the clams can be magical, and in this recipe, that is exactly what happens.

Follow the instructions on page 42 to make the Multipurpose Pasta Dough. While the pasta dough is resting, prepare your clams.

Clean your clams in cold running water to remove any outer sand or grit. In a large bowl, combine the water, ice and salt. Stir to dissolve and place the clams in the bowl. Refrigerate the clams, or add more ice and let them sit, for 20 minutes or up to an hour. This will help dislodge any sand inside the clams. Next, remove the clams from the water, and they are ready to use.

Next, roll and cut your pasta. For fettuccine, take your pasta sheets and cut them into strips approximately ¼ inch (6 mm) wide, then set aside.

For the sauce, coat a Dutch oven or large pan with olive oil over medium heat. Add the onions and sweat them, stirring often, for 3 to 5 minutes, or until fragrant and translucent but not brown. Add the garlic for another 30 seconds, stirring.

Increase the heat to high, put the clams in the pan with the wine and bay leaf and cover. Cook until the liquid is rapidly boiling, then reduce the heat to medium-high. The clams will open when they are done. This will take 5 to 8 minutes, depending on the size of the clams. Once done, reduce the heat to low while you remove the clams with a slotted spoon from the liquid. Set the clams aside to cool enough to handle. Turn the heat back up to medium and continue to reduce the liquid by about a third. Doing this over medium instead of high heat takes a little longer, 6 to 8 minutes, but develops a better flavor.

(continued)

Fettuccine
1 recipe Multipurpose Pasta Dough (page 42)

Salt, for boiling water

Clams
50 littleneck clams in shells (about 3 lb [1.4 kg]; see Notes)

8 cups (1.9 L) water

1 cup (64 g) ice

¼ cup (64 g) kosher salt

Sauce
2 tbsp (30 ml) extra virgin olive oil

½ cup (110 g) finely chopped onions

6 cloves garlic, peeled and chopped fine

1¾ cups (414 ml) dry white wine

1 bay leaf

Fettuccine with White Wine Clam Sauce (Continued)

While the sauce reduces, you can remove the clams from their shells and discard the shells. Optionally, you can keep some clams in one or both of their shells for presentation.

Once the sauce has reduced, carefully pour the liquid into a cup and reserve, discarding the bay leaf. Let this liquid sit for a few minutes, as any unwanted grit will sink to the bottom.

Wipe down the pan and, over medium heat, add back the reserved liquid to the pan making sure not to pour in any sand from the clams that may have settled to the bottom. Often, there is very little or none if you cleaned the clams properly, but this will ensure you don't have any in the final dish. Add the oregano, parsley and thyme and simmer the sauce while you begin heating a large pot of water to cook the pasta.

Bring a large pot of well-salted water, about 2 tablespoons (36 g) of salt per 6 to 8 quarts (6 to 8 L) of water, to a boil. Once boiling, add the pasta and allow it to cook for 2 to 3 minutes. Take one noodle out and test it for doneness. The pasta should be al dente, meaning it will have a bite, but should not taste like raw flour.

Just before the pasta is done, remove the sauce from the heat and whisk in the butter to create a thin buttery sauce. Add the clams back into the sauce as well as the red pepper flakes, lemon juice, Parmesan, capers and salt. Stir, taste for seasoning and add additional salt if needed.

Drain the pasta, add it to the pan with the sauce and clams and toss to coat. Transfer it to a serving bowl and add some chopped parsley, lemon zest and Parmesan.

Notes

If you are unable to get fresh clams, you can also use 1 pound (454 g) of frozen or canned raw clam meat. If fresh small clams are not available or affordable, I would always choose frozen over canned.

Clams can have a wide variation of saltiness. Just taste the sauce at the end and adjust to your liking as you'll notice there is not a lot of salt added to the sauce itself.

1 tbsp (3 g) chopped fresh oregano

1 tbsp (3 g) chopped fresh parsley

1 tbsp (3 g) chopped fresh thyme

5 tbsp (70 g) unsalted butter

½ tsp crushed red pepper flakes

2 tbsp (30 ml) fresh lemon juice

½ cup (50 g) grated Parmesan cheese

2 tbsp (15 g) capers, rinsed

¼ tsp kosher salt, plus more to taste

Garnish
Finely chopped parsley

Lemon zest (from ½–1 lemon)

Grated Parmesan cheese

Summer Pasta

This recipe is simple, but impeccable. This can be made any time of year, but when cherry tomatoes come into season in the summer, we eat this as often as we can! If you have some special olive oil, this is the time to use it to finish the dish. If you don't, get some! Although this is a simple dish, taking advantage of fresh summer cherry tomatoes you grew yourself or bought at a farmers' market and outstanding olive oil will make it seem like a gourmet experience. As a side note, cherry tomatoes work the best in this dish, as opposed to chopped tomatoes or grape tomatoes.

Follow the instructions on page 42 to make the Multipurpose Pasta Dough. While the pasta dough is resting, prepare the rest of your ingredients.

Cut the mozzarella and tomatoes in half. Next, stack the basil leaves, then roll them like a cigar and cut to achieve thin ribbons, called chiffonade. Add the remaining ingredients to small separate bowls to easily add to your dish when you are ready to use them.

Next, roll and cut your pasta. For fettuccine, take your pasta sheets and cut them into strips approximately ¼ inch (6 mm) wide, then set aside.

Bring a large pot of well-salted water, about 2 tablespoons (36 g) of salt per 6 to 8 quarts (6 to 8 L) of water, to a boil. Once boiling, add the pasta and allow it to cook for 2 to 3 minutes. Take one noodle out and test it for doneness. The pasta should be al dente, meaning it will have a bite, but should not taste like raw flour.

While the pasta is cooking, preheat a large skillet over medium heat. Once hot, add the olive oil—this doesn't have to be your "best" olive oil, but should be good for cooking.

When the pasta is ready, remove it from the water and put it in the skillet to coat with oil. Don't worry if some pasta water ends up in the pan, a few tablespoons (30 ml) maximum. Next, reduce the heat to medium-low, add the tomatoes and heat through for about 2 minutes. Then, add the crushed red pepper flakes and stir.

To finish the dish, remove the pan from the heat, and add the mozzarella and basil directly to the pan. Toss to combine. Immediately transfer the pasta to a serving bowl and add your best extra virgin olive oil and Parmesan. Taste and add finishing salt if needed. Add some extra crushed red pepper flakes and fresh basil, if desired and serve. You can always add more of your favorite olive oil from Italy at the end as well!

Serves: 4

1 recipe Multipurpose Pasta Dough (page 42), for fettuccine

Salt, for boiling water

8 oz (226 g) fresh ciliegine mozzarella

1 pint (300 g) cherry tomatoes

10 large basil leaves, plus more if desired

2 tbsp (30 ml) olive oil

1 tbsp (6 g) crushed red pepper flakes, plus more if desired

2 tbsp (30 ml) best-quality extra virgin olive oil (your favorite)

3 tbsp (18 g) grated Parmesan cheese

1 tsp sea salt or finishing salt of your choice (optional)

Beet and Goat Cheese Ravioli with Peas and Lemon Mint Cream Sauce

This recipe combines some of our favorite spring flavors with fall flavors for a brilliant dish that can be made any time of the year! Although some of the ingredients here are seasonal, they typically can be found throughout the year in grocery stores. The mint in the cream sauce is subtle but balances out the rich flavors of the beet and goat cheese filling for a light and refreshing meal!

Preheat the oven to 400°F (205°C).

To make the filling, start by trimming the top and bottom off the beet and washing it thoroughly. Wrap it in foil and add ½ teaspoon of water into the foil with the beet. Place it in a baking dish and roast it for about 1 hour. The beet should be tender and easily pierced with a fork when it is done.

While the beet roasts, make 1 recipe of Multipurpose Pasta Dough (page 42). While the pasta dough is resting, make your filling.

Remove the beet from the oven and allow it to cool briefly, then peel and roughly chop it into small pieces. Add the beet to a food processor with the goat cheese, mascarpone, salt, white wine vinegar, white balsamic vinegar, thyme and pepper. Pulse the mixture to combine, but don't blend until completely smooth. Some slight texture from the beets is preferable in the filling. Transfer to a bowl or piping bag and set aside in the fridge while you roll out your pasta sheets.

Line a baking sheet with parchment paper and lightly dust it with flour.

Next, roll out your pasta. Do not let your ravioli dough sit for too long before filling it, or it may get too dry and crack when you try to make your ravioli. We often roll out one sheet at a time, then fill and cut the ravioli from that one sheet and set them aside.

(continued)

Serves: 4

Filling
1 small (3½-oz [100-g]) beet

⅓ cup (100 g) goat cheese

5 tbsp (50 g) mascarpone cheese

1 tsp kosher salt

½ tsp white wine vinegar

½ tsp white balsamic vinegar

½ tsp finely chopped lemon thyme or regular thyme

⅛ tsp black pepper

Ravioli
1 recipe Multipurpose Pasta Dough (page 42)

Salt, for boiling water

Beet and Goat Cheese Ravioli with Peas and Lemon Mint Cream Sauce (Continued)

To make the ravioli, lay your pasta sheet flat on a lightly floured work surface. Add about 1 to 2 teaspoons of filling about 2 to 2½ inches (5 to 6 cm) apart on half of the sheet. Fold the sheet in half onto your filling scoops, bringing the two short edges together. Carefully press the sheets together around each scoop of filling. Press out as much air as possible. Next, use a ravioli cutter or a knife to cut your sheet into 3 x 3–inch (7½ x 7½–cm) squares, then set the ravioli aside on your parchment-lined baking sheet. Once all the ravioli are made, they can sit at room temperature or in the refrigerator, if made in advance, until the sauce is ready.

The peas for the sauce cook separately and can be done in advance. In a saucepan, bring just enough water to cover the peas to a boil with a pinch or two of salt. Prepare a bowl of ice water. Add the peas to the boiling water and cover. After 2½ minutes, remove the peas and place them in the ice water to stop the cooking process. Once the peas have cooled, about 2 to 3 minutes, remove them to a bowl and set aside.

To make the lemon mint cream sauce, heat the butter over medium heat in a large saucepan until it's bubbling. Add the flour and stir, reducing the heat to medium-low. Cook for several minutes, stirring often. Do not brown the flour. The aroma of raw flour should gradually disappear after 5 to 7 minutes. Next, thoroughly whisk the cream into the flour to remove any lumps, then turn the heat to medium or medium-high. Add the mint leaves, lemon juice, pepper and salt. Bring the cream to a boil, then reduce the heat to medium and cook for 12 to 15 minutes, until the sauce is thickened to the desired consistency. Remove the mint leaves and turn the heat to low.

While the sauce thickens, bring a large pot of well-salted water, about 2 tablespoons (36 g) of salt per 6 to 8 quarts (6 to 8 L) of water, to a boil. Once boiling, add the ravioli and allow it to cook for 2 to 3 minutes. They will float once they are done. Once all the ravioli are floating, remove them with a slotted spoon from the water.

Right before you plate the ravioli, add the precooked peas back to the sauce. Plate the ravioli and spoon the finished sauce over the top. Finish with some freshly grated Parmesan cheese.

Sauce

1 cup (200 g) fresh peas

1 tsp unsalted butter

2 tsp (6 g) all-purpose flour

2 cups (473 ml) heavy cream

8 fresh mint leaves

Juice of 1 lemon
(about ⅛ cup [30 ml])

⅛ tsp white pepper

2 tsp (12 g) kosher salt

Garnish

Freshly grated Parmesan cheese

Butternut Squash Ravioli with Parmesan Sage Cream Sauce

Anytime this dish is on a menu at a restaurant, Angela will order it. Guaranteed! This is one of her absolute favorite dishes, so we recreated it to have at home whenever she wanted. According to Angela, this version is by far the best that she has had! The toppings here should be treated like main ingredients, meaning, you should not skip them unless you have some type of aversion or allergy. If you've never had toasty buttered bread crumbs on pasta, you will be in for a treat. The crispy fried sage leaves add amazing texture to the dish, and they look beautiful as well!

Preheat the oven to 400°F (205°C) and line a baking sheet with parchment paper.

To make the filling, start by slicing a medium butternut squash lengthwise and scooping the seeds out. Place the halves cut side down on the baking sheet. Roast for 45 minutes, or until you can pierce the squash with a fork without much resistance.

While the butternut squash roasts, make 1 recipe of Multipurpose Pasta Dough (page 42). While the pasta dough is resting, finish making the filling.

Remove the squash from the oven and allow it to cool enough to handle. Remove the skin and add the butternut squash flesh to a food processor or blender. Blend until smooth. Use 1 cup (210 g) for the ravioli filling.

Thoroughly mix all remaining filling ingredients with the butternut squash puree in a bowl. If making this in advance, cover and place it in the fridge to use within one week.

Line a baking sheet with parchment paper and lightly dust with flour.

To make the ravioli, lay your pasta sheet flat on a lightly floured work surface. Add about 1 to 2 teaspoons (5 to 10 g) of filling about 2 to 2½ inches (5 to 6 cm) apart on half of the sheet. Fold the sheet in half onto your filling scoops, bringing the two short edges together. Carefully press the sheets together around each scoop of filling. Press out as much air as possible. Next, use a ravioli cutter or a knife to cut your sheet into 3 x 3–inch (7½ x 7½–cm) squares, then set the ravioli aside on your parchment-lined baking sheet. Your ravioli can sit at room temperature or in the refrigerator, if made in advance, until the sauce is ready.

(continued)

Serves: 4

Filling

1 medium butternut squash

1½ cups (360 g) ricotta cheese

⅓ cup (32 g) grated Parmesan cheese

⅛ tsp each salt and pepper

½ tsp crushed red pepper flakes

1 large egg

¼ cup (26 g) toasted bread crumbs

Ravioli

1 recipe Multipurpose Pasta Dough (page 42)

Salt, for boiling water

Butternut Squash Ravioli with Parmesan Sage Cream Sauce (Continued)

Next, make the pasta toppings. Add the butter to a skillet over medium-low heat. When the butter is done bubbling, add the bread crumbs. Stir often. You can turn the heat up a little, and when the bread crumbs have turned golden brown, remove them from the heat. They will turn toasty brown very quickly, so be careful here. Remove to a plate to cool.

Use the same skillet you used for the bread crumbs and heat over medium heat. Add the thin slices of prosciutto. They will crisp up quite quickly, so you only want them on for 5 to 10 seconds per side. Remove to a cutting board and chop finely.

Add the oil to a small saucepan. It should be about ½ inch (1.3 cm) deep, so add or subtract oil depending on the size of your saucepan. Heat over medium-high heat for a few minutes. Pick out some large, nice sage leaves you want to crisp. Place a tester sage leaf in the oil. It should sizzle right away but not discolor. If it discolors, your oil is too hot, and you will need to turn down the heat. If it does not sizzle right away, your oil is not hot enough and you will need to turn it up.

The sage leaves will be in the oil for 5 to 8 seconds. Once done, move them to paper towels to drain the oil. The sage leaves should be a darker green, not brown, and not limp and greasy. If you take them out and they are greasy and limp, put them back in the oil for 2 to 4 seconds, and they should bubble and crisp as soon as they hit the oil.

Once all the steps above are complete, start the sauce by adding the cream, ripped sage leaves and peppercorns to a medium saucepan. Bring to a simmer and hold until the cream has reduced by half, stirring with a rubber spatula every couple of minutes to make sure it doesn't stick to the pan. This will take 15 to 20 minutes, so be patient and allow it to reduce properly.

While the sauce reduces, bring a large pot of well-salted water, about 2 tablespoons (36 g) of salt per 6 to 8 quarts (6 to 8 L) of water, to a boil.

When the sauce has reduced, strain the solids using a fine sieve and return the strained sauce to the saucepan. Add the Parmesan, chopped sage, vinegar and salt. Stir and simmer for 2 minutes. Taste and add more salt, if necessary.

Once the pot of water is boiling, add the ravioli and allow it to cook for 2 to 3 minutes. They will float once they are done. Once all the ravioli are floating, remove them with a slotted spoon from the water to serving plates and add the sauce and toppings.

Toppings (see Note)

2 tbsp (28 g) unsalted butter

¼ cup (30 g) bread crumbs

3 thin slices prosciutto

3 tbsp (44 ml) vegetable oil

8–10 sage leaves

Sauce

1½ cups (355 ml) heavy cream

3 sage leaves, ripped in half

4 each white and black peppercorns, whole

1½ cups (150 g) grated Parmesan Cheese

2 tbsp (7 g) chopped fresh sage

¼ tsp white wine vinegar

⅛ tsp kosher salt, plus more to taste

Note

The toppings can be made up to an hour or so in advance and set aside until you are ready to make the pasta.

Ricotta Spinach Cannelloni with Grandma's Sunday Sauce

Slow Italian cooking is a labor of love, and a dish like this is one that we make on weekends. Sundays are for pasta-making and Grandma's Sunday Sauce! This dish is absolutely worth making with homemade pasta sheets, but of course we feel that homemade pasta elevates every dish.

Begin by making Grandma's Sunday Sauce following the directions on page 145, and keep warm on low. If you made the sauce in advance, add 3 cups (710 ml) to a sauce pan and simmer while you prepare the rest of the recipe. Alternatively, if you do not have time to make the sauce, you can make the meatballs with the Quick Tomato Sauce (page 114) instead.

While the sauce simmers, add the oil in a skillet over medium-high heat. Add the onion and sauté, stirring for about 5 minutes, or until the onion is translucent. Remove the onion to a bowl, add the ground beef to the skillet and turn the heat up slightly. Cook the beef until it is browned, then return the onion to the pan. Add the salt and pepper, stir thoroughly, add the mixture to about 3 cups (710 ml) of Grandma's Sunday Sauce and set aside.

To make the filling, add the water to a shallow skillet over high heat. Once the water is hot, add the spinach and toss for 20 seconds, until slightly wilted. Strain and place on a towel. Gently squeeze out excess moisture. Allow the spinach to cool and dry.

Chop the basil and spinach somewhere between medium and finely chopped, then add to a bowl with the ricotta, egg, Parmesan, mozzarella, red pepper flakes, salt, pepper and nutmeg. Mix until thoroughly combined and set aside while you roll and cut your pasta dough.

(continued)

Serves: 4–6

Sauce

3 cups (710 ml) Grandma's Sunday Sauce (page 145; see Notes)

1 tbsp (15 ml) olive oil

½ cup (80 g) small-diced onion

¾ lb (340 g) ground beef

1 tsp kosher salt

Pinch of black pepper

Filling

¼ cup (59 ml) water

1 cup (60 g) packed raw spinach

½ cup (20 g) packed fresh basil

16 oz (454 g) ricotta

1 large egg

¼ cup (25 g) grated Parmesan cheese

3 oz (85 g) shredded mozzarella

1 tbsp (5 g) crushed red pepper flakes

1 tsp kosher salt

½ tsp black pepper

⅛ tsp ground nutmeg

Ricotta Spinach Cannelloni with Grandma's Sunday Sauce (Continued)

If using fresh pasta dough, follow the instructions for making Multipurpose Pasta Dough on page 42. To make cannelloni sheets, cut the sheets of pasta into rectangles measuring 5 x 4 inches (12.5 x 10 cm). Then lay the cannelloni rectangles out on a flat surface and place the filling along the center, 3 to 4 tablespoons (75 g) of filling per rectangle. Roll the long ends together so that they overlap about ½ inch (1.3 cm). If there is space on the ends of the tubes once you roll them, add extra filling so that the cannelloni are filled completely.

Next, preheat the oven to 350°F (177°C).

In a 9 x 13–inch (23 x 33–cm) baking dish, add approximately 1 cup (225 g) of sauce and make sure to spread it so the dish is completely covered. You want to provide a thin layer between the dish and the bottom of the cannelloni so they don't stick to the dish.

Then add each tube in a single layer to the baking dish and cover with the remaining sauce. Cover the dish with foil and bake for 25 to 30 minutes. The sauce should be bubbling on the sides when it is ready. If you do not see the sauce bubbling along the sides, cook for 5 more minutes.

Once bubbling, remove from the oven and add the grated Parmesan cheese and mozzarella to the top. Return the baking dish to the oven and bake for another 10 minutes. Once done, the cheese should be slightly browned on top. You can broil the dish for 1 to 2 additional minutes if you want a bit more color on your cheese. Once the cheese is browned to your liking, remove the dish from the oven and allow it to cool for 10 minutes before serving.

Cannelloni

1 recipe Multipurpose Pasta Dough (page 42; see Notes)

Salt, for boiling water

Toppings

⅓ cup (33 g) grated Parmesan cheese

8 oz (226 g) fresh mozzarella, sliced or torn into smaller pieces

Notes

Alternatively, you can use one 12- to 16-ounce (340- to 454-g) box of pasta tubes, either cannelloni or manicotti shells. If you are using store-bought dried pasta sheets or tubes, follow the cooking directions on the packaging, but only boil for 70 percent of the total time listed. For example, if the instructions say 14 minutes, cook for 9 minutes instead. Remove the parboiled sheets or tubes from the water and set aside until you are ready to add the filling.

The sauce can be made in advance and kept in the fridge for up to a week, or we like to make it in larger quantities and portion it out in containers to freeze. It will keep in the freezer for up to 6 months.

You can also make this dish using Grandma's Sunday Sauce without the meat for a vegetarian option.

Italian Sausage Lasagna

We love a good lasagna, but we are often disappointed by the lack of flavors we find in versions in restaurants, or any take and bake version. For this version, we took our from-scratch approach and gave the entire dish a makeover. The ricotta mixture is the same mixture we use in ravioli and cannelloni filling, the béchamel is so creamy and packed with flavor and the Sausage Sauce (page 146) takes this lasagna to a whole new level. Of course, homemade pasta makes this lasagna something truly special that you can't get in stores.

Follow the instructions on page 42 for the Multipurpose Pasta Dough, and while the pasta dough is resting, make the Sausage Sauce (page 146) and your filling.

To make the filling, add the water to a shallow skillet over high heat. Once the water is hot, add the spinach and toss for 20 seconds, until slightly wilted. Strain and place the spinach on a towel. Gently squeeze out excess moisture. Allow the spinach to cool and dry.

Chop the basil and spinach somewhere between medium and finely chopped, then add to a bowl with the ricotta, egg, Parmesan, mozzarella, red pepper flakes, salt, pepper and nutmeg. Mix until thoroughly combined and set aside while you roll and cut your pasta dough.

For lasagna sheets, leave your pasta sheets whole, then cut them to the length of your baking dish and trim the width as needed.

To make the béchamel, first warm the milk in a small saucepan to just under a simmer. In another saucepan, melt the butter over medium heat. Add the flour to the butter and whisk constantly to combine without browning the flour. Add the milk gradually, while whisking until a smooth consistency is reached and there are no lumps. Cook over medium-low heat for 10 to 15 minutes, whisking often. Add nutmeg and salt to taste.

(continued)

Lasagna Sheets

1 recipe Multipurpose Pasta Dough (page 42; see Notes)

Salt, for boiling water

Sausage Sauce

1 recipe Sausage Sauce (page 146)

Ricotta and Spinach Filling

¼ cup (59 ml) water

1 cup (60 g) packed raw spinach

½ cup (20 g) packed fresh basil

16 oz (454 g) ricotta

1 large egg

¼ cup (25 g) grated Parmesan cheese

3 oz (85 g) shredded mozzarella

1 tbsp (5 g) crushed red pepper flakes

1 tsp kosher salt

½ tsp black pepper

⅛ tsp ground nutmeg

Béchamel Sauce

3⅓ cups (789 ml) whole milk

4 tbsp (56 g) unsalted butter

⅓ cup plus 1 tbsp (50 g) all-purpose flour

⅛ tsp fresh ground nutmeg, plus more to taste

½ tsp kosher salt, plus more to taste

Italian Sausage Lasagna (Continued)

Preheat your oven to 375°F (190°C) and assemble your lasagna, starting with a thin layer of olive oil on the bottom and sides of a 9 x 13–inch (23 x 33–cm) baking dish. Add a layer each of pasta, then sauce, béchamel and ricotta mixture. Lastly sprinkle with Parmesan. You will use about a third of each of these ingredients but use your best judgment to equally distribute them throughout the dish as you create each layer.

Repeat the layers until your dish is full, with the top being a layer of pasta and a thin layer of sauce. Sprinkle the top with more Parmesan if desired, add mozzarella and a few basil leaves and cook in the oven for 40 to 50 minutes, or until bubbly, and the center is hot, approximately 170°F (77°C).

Remove from the oven and let stand for 10 to 15 minutes before serving.

Notes

Homemade Ricotta (page 154) can be made ahead of time or while you make the sauce. Alternatively, you can buy ricotta.

Homemade pasta can be made up to 6 hours before and kept in the fridge until you are ready to assemble your lasagna.

Fresh pasta does not need to be parboiled before assembling your lasagna. If you are using store-bought dried pasta sheets, follow the cooking directions on the packaging, but only boil for 70 percent of the total time listed. For example, if the instructions say 14 minutes, cook for 9 minutes instead. Remove parboiled sheets from the water and set aside until you are ready to assemble the lasagna.

Assembly and Toppings

Olive oil, for the baking dish

¾ cup (75 g) freshly grated Parmesan cheese, divided, plus more if desired

4 oz (56 g) fresh mozzarella, torn or cut into ⅛" (3-mm) discs

Fresh basil leaves

Lemon Parmesan Orzo

This orzo is cooked in a unique way, which results in its own sauce, and is quite easy and tastes incredible. It may sound like a summer dish, but this is enjoyable any time of the year. Orzo is one of the only pastas we don't make fresh at home, but it really works well in this recipe. The inspiration for this dish came from my parents, who often serve this with spicy shrimp, but it is great with just about anything!

Begin by heating the olive oil in a high-sided sauté pan, skillet or saucepan over medium heat. Add the onion and sweat it for 1 to 2 minutes. You are not trying to brown the onion, so adjust the heat as needed.

Next, turn the heat down to medium-low and add the garlic, stirring often, for another 30 seconds to a minute, until the onion is translucent and the garlic is fragrant. Once the onion and garlic are done, add the chicken stock, cover and bring to a boil.

Once the liquid is boiling, remove the lid, add the orzo and bring the contents back to a boil. Then reduce the heat to low and replace the lid.

Cook the orzo, removing the lid to stir every few minutes and making sure the orzo is simmering gently, but isn't sticking to the bottom. Add a little water if your orzo looks too dry and begins to stick throughout the cooking process.

The total cooking time should be about 15 minutes, but after 12 minutes, taste the pasta for doneness. The orzo should absorb most of the liquid and still be al dente, or have a little bite.

When the orzo is done, turn the heat off, add the Parmesan and lemon juice and stir to combine completely. Finally, add salt and pepper to taste.

Serves: 4

2 tbsp (30 ml) olive oil

¾ cup (40 g) chopped yellow onion

1 clove garlic, minced

2 cups (473 ml) chicken stock

1 cup (230 g) dried orzo pasta

½ cup (50 g) grated Parmesan cheese

¼ cup (59 ml) lemon juice

Salt and pepper, to taste

Parmesan Risotto

This classic dish goes well with any meat dish, but especially osso-buco or other stewed or braised dishes. Risotto is much easier to make than most people think and has such a rich and satisfying taste. We have used several different risotto rices, and our favorite is carnaroli. It releases the perfect amount of starch and produces a creamy risotto with the perfect "bite" to the rice when done. There are so many variants to risotto as far as flavoring and we have added our favorites in this book.

Warm the chicken stock in a saucepan over medium-low heat. Keep it at a very warm or hot temperature below boiling.

Next, heat a large, deep skillet or pan over medium heat until hot, then add the olive oil. Add the onion and reduce the heat to medium-low. Sauté until the onion is translucent without browning the onion. Add the first 2 tablespoons (28 g) of butter. Once it has melted, increase the heat to medium. Then add the rice to the skillet and coat the grains of rice with the butter. Sauté for 2 minutes.

Add the wine and cook until it is almost completely absorbed. Stir often with a rubber spatula or wooden spoon so that the rice doesn't stick to the pan. After 2 to 3 minutes, once the wine has absorbed, start adding the hot stock to the rice, one ladle or about ½ to ¾ cup (118 to 177 ml), at a time. Stir often.

Continue adding the stock as it gets absorbed by the rice, a ladle at a time, stirring often to prevent the rice from sticking to the bottom of the pan or browning. Be sure to wait until all the stock is absorbed by the rice before adding more—this is a key element in making a successful risotto. Adjust the heat lower, if necessary, during this process if your liquid absorbs too quickly and your rice begins to stick or brown.

After about two thirds of the stock has been added and absorbed—around 18 to 20 minutes of cooking—taste the rice for doneness. The texture should be firm but done, not mushy and not crunchy. You may not need all of the stock. If you run out of stock, you can use hot water to add to the rice to finish it off.

Once the rice is done, remove it from the heat and stir in the remaining 2 tablespoons (28 g) of butter, salt, pepper and Parmesan cheese.

Serve garnished with parsley and additional grated Parmesan cheese.

Serves: 4–6

6–8 cups (1.4–1.9 L) unsalted chicken stock

2–3 tbsp (30–45 ml) olive oil

1 small (3-oz [85-g]) onion, chopped fine

4 tbsp (56 g) unsalted butter, divided

2 cups (360 g) risotto rice (carnaroli or arborio)

½ cup (118 ml) dry white wine (pinot grigio or similar)

¼ tsp kosher salt

¼ tsp black pepper

1 cup (90 g) grated Parmesan cheese

Garnish
Chopped parsley

Freshly grated Parmesan cheese

Note
To make saffron risotto, simply add 1 teaspoon of saffron threads to the stock. The unique flavor and aroma of saffron elevate this risotto to new heights.

Sherry Mushroom Risotto

These flavorful mushrooms are one of our favorite additions to risotto. Although mushroom risotto is traditional in Italian cuisine, cooking the mushrooms separately with the tarragon and incorporating them at the end adds a different twist. The risotto ends up having a different flavor profile than the traditional version that, in our opinion, makes this a more exciting dish, whether eaten alone or as a side!

Make the Parmesan Risotto Recipe following the instructions on page 74.

Once the risotto has been cooking for about 15 minutes, begin the mushrooms. In a skillet large enough to not crowd the mushrooms—larger is better—heat the butter over medium heat. When the butter has melted, add the mushrooms, salt and pepper, and cook them for 5 to 7 minutes, until they absorb the butter and start to brown. Add the green onion, sherry and wine, then increase the heat to medium-high and reduce the liquid by half. This will take 3 to 7 minutes (see Note). Add the chopped tarragon, cook for another minute and taste for seasoning.

Mix it into your risotto and serve with extra tarragon for garnish.

Note

The size of your skillet or pan will dramatically affect how much time it takes to reduce liquids and cook the mushrooms. If you use a 12-inch (30-cm) skillet for the mushrooms, the sherry and wine may evaporate in as little as 3 minutes, but in a smaller skillet, just large enough to hold the mushrooms in a single layer, this may take as much as 6 or 7 minutes.

Serves: 4–6

1 recipe Parmesan Risotto (page 74)

3 tbsp (42 g) unsalted butter

8 oz (226 g) small to medium cremini mushrooms, sliced about ¼" (6 mm) thick

Pinch of kosher salt

Pinch of pepper

2 tbsp (11 g) thinly sliced green onion

⅓ cup (79 ml) sherry

¼ cup (59 ml) dry red wine

2 tarragon sprigs, leaves only, chopped, plus more to garnish

Asparagus, Pea and Pine Nut Risotto

This is a great way to lighten up risotto for spring or summer eating, but it is great any time. The asparagus tips cook in the risotto, adding their flavor to the dish.

1 recipe Parmesan Risotto
(page 74)

¾ cup (100 g) asparagus tips

¾ cup (170 g) fresh green peas

½ cup (68 g) pine nuts

Make the Parmesan Risotto Recipe following the instructions on page 74, but halfway through, after 10 to 12 minutes, add the asparagus tips to the rice and allow them to cook as you cook the rice.

The peas cook separately and can be done in advance. In a saucepan with a steamer basket, bring just a small amount of water to a boil without submerging the bottom of the steamer basket. Add the peas and cover. After 2 minutes, remove the peas and set aside. Add the peas to the risotto with the last ladle of stock.

The pine nuts can be made ahead of time by heating them up in a dry pan over medium heat until they start to toast. Shake the pan often to turn the pine nuts over. This takes about 3 minutes, and you will see them start to release their oils and begin to brown. Remove them to a bowl and mix the pine nuts into the risotto before serving.

BY LAND OR BY SEA

Meat and Seafood Dishes to Elevate Your Meals from Sunday Dinners to Date Nights and Everything in Between

The roots of my family are in the region of Abruzzo, which has a large coastline to the east and mountainous and hilly areas to the west. However, the province where both my grandfather's and grandmother's families are from is L'Aquila, which is landlocked and very mountainous. This is likely why poultry, beef, veal, lamb and pork were much more prominent than seafood in our family recipes! I just know my dad won't eat fish and, therefore, it was not a staple in my immediate family growing up. I'm lucky that I love all foods, and I will happily try a dish of any protein if the dish is made well!

The geography of Italy is unique, giving access to so many treasures that form the foundation of such an important cuisine. In our travels all across Italy, the various proteins we were lucky enough to eat left us wanting to go back as often as possible. Practicality rules the day, however, so wherever you are from, the best way to enjoy anything is to find the freshest, most local providers that you can and give it a try. Many times, the artisan fishermen, ranchers and farmers that are local will provide you with things that will make others jealous. Just find them!

If it is beef, pork, lamb, poultry, sausage or seafood you crave, read on! These next recipes have been developed with love and care that can make your menu a special one.

Chianti Braised Beef with Creamy Cheese and Spinach Polenta

We love to make this Chianti braised beef during the winter and especially around the holidays when our families are visiting. It takes several hours to cook properly, but the result is an incredibly decadent and heartwarming dish that never disappoints. In fact, it is so good that you will make plans to eat the leftovers, if there are any, before you finish your meal. Some may even prefer it the following day, as the flavors will have had time to spend the night together and develop a love for one another.

We paired the braised beef here with a creamy cheese and spinach polenta to complement the rich beef and sauce. The richness and creaminess of both will have you dreaming of a winter's night by the fireplace in the mountains of Italy. But you can certainly serve this beef with mashed potatoes, risotto, pasta or a number of starches and make it a fantastic meal. We like to pair this with a nice Chianti Classico to round out the meal with the perfect sip.

Preheat the oven to 450°F (232°C).

Heat a Dutch oven or heavy pot over medium-high heat. Add the olive oil and pancetta. Cook for 3 to 5 minutes, until the pancetta has rendered its fat and has browned, then remove it with a slotted spoon to a large bowl.

Season the beef with the salt and pepper. Add the beef to the Dutch oven where you cooked the pancetta over medium-high heat and brown in batches, 2 to 4 depending on your pot size. If the pan seems dry, add a little more olive oil. Do not overcrowd the Dutch oven. Once the meat has browned on all sides, approximately 5 minutes per batch, remove it with a slotted spoon and set it aside in the bowl with the pancetta.

At this point, you may have developed a good amount of "fond," or browned bits, in your pot, and we want to make sure we incorporate all that flavor. With the heat on medium-high to high, add the water, wine or stock and scrape off the fond with a wooden spoon.

Add the red onion, yellow onion, celery and carrots to the Dutch oven. Stir often to brown the vegetables, adjusting the heat as necessary. If the pot is too dry, you can add a small amount of oil. Once the vegetables are browned, turn the heat to medium-low and add the garlic and tomato paste, stirring to incorporate. Cook for about a minute, until the garlic is fragrant.

Serves: 6–8

Braised Beef

2 tbsp (30 ml) olive oil or grapeseed oil (not extra virgin olive oil), plus more as needed

6 oz (170 g) pancetta, small dice

3 lb (1.4 kg) lean beef, cut into 1–1½" (2.5–4-cm) cubes

1 tbsp (18 g) kosher salt

1 tsp pepper

¼ cup (59 ml) water, wine or stock

1 medium (5-oz [142-g]) red onion, diced

1 medium (5-oz [142-g]) yellow onion, diced

2 (2-oz [57-g]) ribs celery, finely sliced

2 medium (4-oz [113-g]) carrots, small dice

4 cloves garlic, minced

3 tbsp (42 g) tomato paste

(continued)

Chianti Braised Beef with Creamy Cheese and Spinach Polenta (Continued)

Return the beef and pancetta to the pot with the vegetables and sprinkle it with the flour. Put the pot into the preheated oven, uncovered, for 5 minutes. After 5 minutes, remove the pot, stir and return for another 5 minutes. Next, remove the pot and place it on the stovetop over medium heat and turn the oven down to 350°F (177°C).

Immediately add the Chianti, stirring and scraping any fond with a wooden spoon or spatula. Once incorporated, add the stock, bay leaf, sage, thyme and oregano and stir. Bring to a gentle simmer and place the pot into the oven to cook, covered, for about 20 minutes.

After 20 minutes, remove the pot from the oven, stir and scrape the bottom to make sure that nothing is sticking, then stir in the balsamic vinegar.

Put the pot back into the 350°F (177°C) oven for 2 hours, covered.

Approximately 20 minutes before your braised beef is done, begin the polenta.

Heat a large skillet over medium-high heat. When the pan is hot, add ¼ cup (59 ml) of water and the spinach. Move the spinach around with tongs for 15 to 20 seconds—it will wilt quickly. Remove the spinach from the pan and let it dry and cool on a towel. Wring out as much water from the spinach as possible, then chop it and set aside.

Bring the stock and 2 cups (473 ml) of water to a gentle boil in a large pot, then add the salt. Add the polenta, about ½ cup (80 g) at a time, while stirring or whisking. Once the polenta is incorporated into the pot, reduce the heat to low and cook for about 20 minutes, or until the polenta is the texture you wish. The polenta should be tender but with some texture and relatively thick. If it is too thick, you can add some water or stock to thin the consistency. Stir often during the 20 minutes to prevent sticking or burning on the bottom of the pot.

Remove the pot of polenta from the heat and add the spinach, butter, milk, Parmesan, basil, parsley and white pepper. Stir to incorporate and taste to see if you need to add salt. Garnish with chopped parsley, if desired, and serve alongside the braised beef.

Once the beef is done, remove the pot from the oven, stir and serve with chopped parsley as a garnish, if desired.

2 tbsp (17 g) all-purpose flour

1 (25-oz [740-ml]) bottle Chianti Classico

2 cups (473 ml) beef stock

1 bay leaf

2 tsp (2 g) rough chopped fresh sage

1 tbsp (3 g) rough chopped fresh thyme

1 tbsp (3 g) rough chopped fresh oregano

1 tbsp (15 ml) balsamic vinegar

Parsley, to garnish

Polenta

2½ cups (591 ml) water, divided, plus more as needed

2 cups (60 g) fresh spinach

2½ cups (591 ml) beef stock or broth

1 tsp kosher salt, plus more to taste

1½ cups (240 g) polenta

6 tbsp (84 g) unsalted butter

¾ cup (177 ml) whole milk

⅔ cup (68 g) grated Parmesan cheese

3 basil leaves, finely chopped

3 tbsp (12 g) finely chopped fresh parsley, plus more to garnish (optional)

¼ tsp white pepper

Salt-Baked Branzino with Tarragon Tomato Cream Sauce

This is one of those dishes that most people will try at a restaurant but definitely not try at home. Don't be intimidated—it's not that difficult. While on a work trip to Italy, Angela ordered one and raved about it nonstop, so of course I had to try to recreate it for her at home. We could not believe just how simple, yet amazing it was, and it has since become one of those dishes we make for guests when we are really trying to impress, but not spend hours preparing a meal. It may not be as easy as making scrambled eggs or ice cubes, but this truly is a very easy dish with an impressive presentation. The salt-baked cooking method results in an absolutely spectacular fish texture and flavor, and cooking a fish in salt is so much more than flair for tableside presentations. Branzino is a great-tasting fish and cooks perfectly in a salt dome.

To top it off, this sauce elevates the entire dish to something you'd expect to eat in a fancy restaurant. This sauce is phenomenal on a variety of white fish, scallops, shrimp or even chicken!

Serves: 2

3 cups (864 g) kosher salt

2 tbsp (4 g) dried thyme

3 large egg whites

1 (2-lb [907-g]) whole branzino

1 lemon, sliced

2 sprigs fresh tarragon

1 sprig fresh rosemary

Preheat the oven to 400°F (204°C).

Line a large roasting pan or sheet pan larger than the fish with parchment paper.

In a large bowl, mix the salt, dried thyme and egg whites with your hands. It should be the consistency of a chunky paste, but not too wet. Set aside.

Remove the fish from the refrigerator and scale it. Gut the fish and remove the gills with kitchen shears. We recommend requesting this at the market before buying to make your life easier.

Cut the dorsal and pectoral fins, and any other that is spiny or might stab you when you are ready to eat.

Stuff the fish cavity with the lemon slices, tarragon and rosemary. Place the fish on the parchment-lined sheet pan.

Put the salt mixture on the fish and press it down, forming a seal that is about ¼ inch (6 mm) thick around the entire fish. There should be no gaps or cracks and the fish should not be visible.

Put the fish in the preheated oven for 20 minutes. Some of the salt mixture may turn a light brown and the salt dome will be quite hard when finished.

(continued)

Salt-Baked Branzino with Tarragon Tomato Cream Sauce (Continued)

While the fish bakes, make the sauce. In a saucepan over medium heat, warm the olive oil until it is hot. Add the onion and cook for about a minute, stirring often, then add the garlic for another 30 seconds. Add the tomatoes and bay leaf and cook for at least 5 minutes, evaporating almost all of the moisture. Add the wine and stir frequently while reducing the wine by 50 percent. This will take at least 5 minutes. Strain the solids out of the sauce, press the tomato and onion mixture to extract all of the juice, and return to the saucepan. Continue reducing over medium heat for about 5 minutes, until the liquid has reduced to about ½ cup (118 ml). Add the cream and reduce again by a third or until the sauce has thickened. This should take 5 to 7 more minutes. Taste for seasoning and add salt and pepper as needed. Stir in the fresh tarragon.

To serve the fish, use a serving spoon to crack the salt dome and remove it from the fish. You want to have enough room to remove the fillets from the Branzino, so scrape the salt away from the fish to the edges of the baking sheet. With a sharp knife, slice the fish through the skin through to the bone where the tail meets the body. You can use your fingers, a knife, a spoon or a spatula to remove the skin from the tail toward the head. The skin should come off very easily without any effort.

Slide your spoon along the spine starting at the tail moving toward the head of the fish where the fillet stops. The meat should easily separate from the spine, but it may be delicate and flaky. Remove to a clean plate. Gently flip the fish over and repeat to remove the opposite fillet.

Serve with the sauce and a few tarragon leaves for garnish, if desired.

Tarragon Tomato Cream Sauce

1 tbsp (15 ml) olive oil

1 small (3-oz [85-g]) onion, diced

1 clove garlic, rough chopped

4–5 medium tomatoes, peeled, seeded and diced

1 bay leaf

1½ cups (355 ml) dry white wine

1½ cups (355 ml) cream

1 tsp kosher salt, plus more to taste

½ tsp black pepper, plus more to taste

2 tsp fresh tarragon, plus more to garnish

Herb-Roasted Shrimp and Spring Gremolata

This dish is full of flavor and also has a sauce worthy of some fresh Italian bread for soaking it all up. The gremolata is lighter and fresher than the traditional version, and it does not have a very assertive garlic punch, making it perfect for a variety of dishes.

For the gremolata, mix the lemon zest, lemon juice, garlic, shallot and red pepper flakes and let it sit in a small bowl while you prepare the rest of the ingredients, about 10 minutes.

Add the finely chopped parsley, mint and cilantro to the lemon juice mixture and combine well. Let it sit at room temperature while you prepare the rest of the dish.

Preheat the oven to 400°F (205°C).

Mix all the ingredients for the seasoning and set aside.

To make the shrimp, once the oven is heated, cut the butter into pieces, add to a 13 x 9–inch (33 x 23–cm) casserole dish and put it in the oven until the butter has melted. This will take 5 to 7 minutes.

Once the butter has melted, remove the dish and add the shrimp, tossing to coat. Sprinkle the shrimp with the seasoning mixture and toss to coat well.

Place the dish in the oven for approximately 15 minutes, or until the shrimp are pink and curling. The shrimp should not curl too tightly in a ball, as that would be an indication that they are overcooked.

Remove the shrimp and butter sauce to a serving plate, sprinkle with the gremolata and serve with some warm Italian bread to sop up the sauce, with orzo or atop pasta such as angel hair or spaghetti.

Note
This shrimp is perfectly accompanied by Lemon Parmesan Orzo (page 73), Multipurpose Pasta Dough (page 42), cut as desired and cooked, or Parmesan Risotto (page 74).

Serves: 4–6

Gremolata
Zest of 2 lemons

Juice of 2 lemons (about 5 tbsp [75 ml])

1 tbsp (2 g) minced garlic

1 tbsp (2 g) minced shallot

¼ tsp crushed red pepper flakes

⅓ cup (20 g) finely chopped parsley

1 tbsp (6 g) finely chopped mint

1 tbsp (1 g) finely chopped cilantro

Seasoning
½ tsp kosher salt

½ tsp dried basil

½ tsp dried oregano

½ tsp dried thyme

1 tsp lemon pepper

¼ tsp finely chopped fresh rosemary

¼ tsp garlic powder

¼ tsp onion powder

⅛ tsp black pepper

1 tsp lemon zest

Shrimp
½ cup (113 g) unsalted butter

1½ lb (680 g) medium/large shrimp, peeled and deveined

Baked Zucchini with Italian Meat Sauce

This one-pot dish is a great way to use an abundance of zucchini when it is in season. This makes quite a bit, but it is exceptional when reheated the next day or two! It works great as a stand-alone dish or can be served with pasta for a heartier meal.

Serves: 8–10

Add the sausage and beef to a large oven-safe Dutch oven or braiser and begin to brown over medium-high to high heat. Cook for 4 to 5 minutes, until the fat starts to render, then add the onion. Continue to cook until the meat is browned and the onion is translucent. This should take 5 to 8 minutes. Stir occasionally to ensure the meat and onion are evenly cooking and break up the meat as you go.

At this point, you can preheat the oven to 375°F (190°C) while you finish the sauce.

Turn the heat to medium and add the whole peeled tomatoes, tomato paste, tomato sauce, diced tomatoes, oregano, garlic powder, pepper and salt to the pot. Cook this down for 15 to 20 minutes, allowing the tomatoes to break down and the sauce to thicken. Taste for seasoning and adjust if necessary, but do not oversalt as you will add Parmesan toward the end.

Once the sauce has thickened, add the zucchini and stir thoroughly. Turn the heat to high for 3 to 4 minutes and then sprinkle with the Parmesan.

Next, place the entire dish, uncovered, in the oven and let it cook for 25 to 30 minutes, or until the zucchini is tender. Serve alone, with crusty Italian bread or with pasta.

1 lb (454 g) hot Italian sausage, casing removed

1 lb (454 g) ground beef

1 large (10-oz [283-g]) onion, chopped

1 (28-oz [794-g]) can whole peeled tomatoes, with juice

1 (6-oz [170-g]) can tomato paste

1 (15-oz [425-g]) can tomato sauce

1 (15-oz [425-g]) can diced tomatoes, with juice

2 tbsp (4 g) dried oregano

2 tsp (3 g) garlic powder

2 tsp (2 g) black pepper

1 tsp kosher salt

2 lb (907 g) zucchini, sliced ¼–⅓" (6–8 mm) thick

1 cup (100 g) grated Parmesan cheese

Crusty Italian bread or pasta, for serving (optional)

Marsala Mushroom, Prosciutto and Spinach Crespelle

Crespelle is the Italian version of French crêpes, but these savory gems are a great change of pace, and they aren't often found on many menus, although they are enjoyed at home. The crespelle can be filled with an endless variety of vegetables, meats or cheeses, but we especially like this wintery combination. If you can find some wild mushrooms, these crespelle are even more flavorful and interesting.

To make the crespelle, first sift the flour into a large bowl, then mix the eggs, milk and melted butter into the flour thoroughly, until there are no clumps. Place the bowl in the fridge for a minimum of 30 minutes or up to an hour.

Place a shallow nonstick 8-inch (20-cm) skillet over low heat. Add the cold butter to the pan and spread it around as it melts so that it covers the bottom. Add a ladle of batter, approximately ¼ cup (59 ml), to the pan. Pick the pan up and tilt it so that the batter covers the bottom of the pan in a thin layer. Allow the crespelle to cook until slightly golden brown, flipping partway through. This will take about 2 minutes on the first side and about 1 minute on the second side. If your crespelle gets too brown, remove the pan briefly from the heat to allow it to cool down before continuing with the next crespelle. Continue to cook until the batter is gone. You should make eight crespelle in total. Set aside.

Next, prepare the filling. Heat a large nonstick skillet over medium heat. Add 2 tablespoons (28 g) of butter to the pan followed by the onion. Allow the onion to cook for 2 minutes, then add the mushrooms and stir to combine. Add the remaining 1 tablespoon (14 g) of butter to the pan and cook for 5 to 6 minutes, stirring occasionally, or until the mushrooms are tender and are a slightly golden-brown color. Then add salt and pepper and stir. Add the marsala and fresh oregano leaves and cook for about 3 more minutes until the marsala has almost completely soaked into the mushrooms. Remove the mushroom and onion mixture from the pan and set aside.

In the same pan over medium-low heat, add the thin slices of prosciutto in a single layer. You may need to do this in batches. Cook each slice for 15 seconds, then remove and set aside. Roughly chop the prosciutto, then combine it with the mushroom mixture and set aside.

(continued)

Serves: 4

Crespelle
¾ cup (100 g) Tipo 00 flour

3 large eggs

¾ cup plus 2 tbsp (89 ml) milk

4 tbsp (59 ml) melted butter

1 tsp cold butter

Filling
3 tbsp (42 g) unsalted butter, divided

¼ cup (34 g) chopped onion

2 cups (135 g) sliced cremini mushrooms

Pinch of kosher salt

Pinch of black pepper

¼ cup (59 ml) marsala

2 tsp (2 g) fresh oregano leaves

3 oz (85 g) thinly sliced prosciutto

Marsala Mushroom, Prosciutto and Spinach Crespelle (Continued)

Turn the heat to medium-high and add the red wine, water and spinach. Toss the spinach to cook evenly in the skillet for 2 minutes, then remove into a colander to strain. Allow the spinach to cool slightly, then squeeze out any excess water using a towel or cheesecloth. Next, chop the spinach and combine it with the mushrooms and prosciutto.

Add the lemon zest and basil to the mushroom, prosciutto and spinach mixture and combine.

To make the béchamel sauce, in a medium saucepan over low heat, add the onion, cloves, bay leaf, nutmeg and milk and allow it to warm for 10 minutes. As the milk mixture warms, heat a large nonstick skillet over medium heat and add the butter. Once the butter is completely melted, add the flour and whisk until smooth. Gently cook over medium heat, stirring occasionally for 3 to 5 minutes.

Next, strain the milk mixture using a fine sieve straight into the flour mixture called the roux, and discard the strained-out solids. Stir to combine thoroughly and increase the heat to medium-high. Continue to stir constantly until the mixture comes to a boil, approximately 2 minutes, then reduce the heat to low. Add the pepper, salt and tomato paste and stir to combine.

To assemble the crespelle, preheat the oven to 350°F (177°C).

Coat the bottom of a 9 x 13-inch (23 x 33-cm) baking dish with olive oil. Add about ¼ cup (30 g) of the mushroom and prosciutto mixture and about 1 tablespoon (15 g) of roughly diced provolone down the middle of each crespelle. Roll the crespelle, then place it in the baking dish.

Top the crespelle with 1 cup (237 ml) of the béchamel and spread it evenly over the top, ensuring that the edges are also coated. Add the grated Parmesan cheese to the top and place in the oven for 15 minutes.

Once done, garnish with basil to serve.

¼ cup (59 ml) dry red wine

¼ cup (59 ml) water

½ lb (227 g) spinach

1 tsp lemon zest (approximately ½ small lemon)

2 tbsp (6 g) chopped fresh basil, plus more to garnish

6 oz (170 g) aged provolone cheese, rough dice

2 tbsp (13 g) grated Parmesan cheese

Béchamel Sauce

½ small (2-oz [57-g]) onion, cut in quarters

2 cloves, whole

1 bay leaf

Pinch of ground nutmeg

1 qt (946 ml) milk

¼ cup (57 g) butter

½ cup (63 g) flour

¼ tsp pepper

1 tbsp (18 g) kosher salt

2 tbsp (28 g) tomato paste

Chicken Piccata with Lemon Caper Butter Sauce

This is a popular dish that can be made with veal as well. But the availability and price of chicken are pretty hard to beat as long as you can infuse some amazing flavors into your dish. And if you want amazing flavors, just make this. You don't need a fancy white wine, but make sure you like the one you're using and it should not be a sweet wine. Pinot Grigio and Sauvignon Blanc work perfectly here.

And don't skip the capers! Many people don't rinse capers before adding them to dishes and then complain about how the capers overwhelm the dish. Well, rinsing the capers is necessary and allows the capers to add the perfect pop of flavor without overpowering the dish.

Preheat the oven to 170°F (77°C).

Season the chicken with salt and pepper. Dredge the chicken in flour, or put the chicken in a plastic bag with the flour and coat completely. Shake off any excess flour.

Melt 2 tablespoons (28 g) of butter in a large stainless skillet over medium heat until the butter has stopped foaming, about 45 seconds, then add the olive oil. Add the chicken and cook for 3 to 4 minutes per side to brown, until almost cooked through. If you do this in two batches, you may need a little more olive oil.

Remove the chicken to a separate ovenproof dish, cover it with aluminum foil and place it in the oven while you make the sauce in the same skillet you used to brown the chicken.

Add the white wine to the pan to deglaze it and scrape the browned bits of fond with a wooden spoon. Reduce the sauce by two-thirds. This will take approximately 5 minutes.

Add the lemon juice and chicken stock and reduce until thickened and you have a sauce consistency, approximately 10 minutes.

Remove the sauce from the heat and whisk in the remaining 8 tablespoons (112 g) of butter, 1 tablespoon (14 g) at a time.

Return the pan to low heat and add the capers, chicken and accumulated chicken juices into the pan with the sauce. Do not raise the heat above low at this point, or your sauce may break. Turn the chicken once and cook briefly, 1 to 2 minutes, in the sauce. Serve alone or over fresh pasta.

*See photo on page 80.

Serves: 4

2 large chicken breasts, sliced in half across, or 4 thin chicken breasts

1 tbsp (18 g) kosher salt

2 tsp black pepper

½ cup (63 g) flour

10 tbsp (140 g) unsalted butter, divided

2 tbsp (30 ml) olive oil

⅔ cup (158 ml) dry white wine

⅓ cup (79 ml) fresh lemon juice

1 cup (237 ml) chicken stock

¼ cup (22 g) capers, rinsed

Veal with Mushroom Tarragon Cream Sauce

To me, veal is hard to pass up. I've ordered it at steakhouses multiple times without regret even if the steaks look amazing! The tarragon cream sauce here brings veal scallopini to a new level that goes well with pasta or any starch.

This is a twist on a traditional veal marsala dish, so if you are a fan of that dish, get ready for this upgraded version!

To make the mushrooms, heat the olive oil over medium heat in a large stainless-steel pan. Add the kosher salt and sliced cremini mushrooms and stir to coat with the oil. Stirring and tossing often, cook for 5 to 8 minutes, or until some browning occurs on the mushrooms. Remove the mushrooms and set aside, but keep the pan, without cleaning it, for the veal.

Preheat your oven to 170°F (77°C).

Pound your veal scallopini with a kitchen mallet to about ⅛ inch (3 mm) to tenderize, then cut it into multiple pieces that can be plated for individual servings, approximately 4 ounces (113 g) per piece. Veal scallopini can get out of control when pounding it out and can take up a whole pan, so it is better to portion it into smaller, more manageable pieces. Season the veal with the salt and pepper and dredge it in the flour. Shake off any excess flour. In the same pan you used for the mushrooms, add the olive oil and begin cooking your veal in batches to brown over medium to medium-high heat for 1 to 2 minutes per side. Remove each batch to an oven-safe pan and set aside. Add additional olive oil to the pan if needed before each batch. Once the veal is done, lightly cover it with foil and place it in the oven to keep warm.

To make the sauce, pour off the excess oil in the pan used for the mushrooms and veal and increase the heat to medium-high. Add the marsala and deglaze the pan, using a wooden spoon to scrape browned bits called fond, off the bottom of the pan. Turn the heat to medium and slowly cook off the alcohol in the marsala for about 3 minutes. Add the cream and return the mushrooms and their juices to the pan. Add the white wine vinegar and simmer over medium or medium-low heat to combine and concentrate the flavors for 7 to 10 minutes, stirring often. Add the tarragon, stir and taste for seasoning. Add additional salt and pepper, to taste.

Serve the veal with the sauce over pasta, rice, vegetables or another starch of your choice.

Serves: 4

Mushrooms

3 tbsp (44 ml) olive oil

½ tsp kosher salt

3 cups sliced cremini mushrooms
(about 6 oz [170 g])

Veal

16 oz (454 g) veal scallopini

½ tsp kosher salt

¼ tsp black pepper

½ cup (63 g) all-purpose flour

3 tbsp (44 ml) olive oil, plus
more as needed

Sauce

¾ cup (177 ml) marsala wine

1 cup (237 ml) heavy cream

1 tsp white wine vinegar

1 tbsp (3 g) chopped fresh
tarragon

Kosher salt, to taste

Pepper, to taste

To Serve

Pasta, rice, vegetables or starch
of choice

Ossobuco alla Perlioni

I absolutely rank ossobuco in its various forms as one of my favorite dishes. After years of fiddling with different variants, we finally settled on this recipe as our favorite. You can sometimes find this made with red wine, and we have had success with that, but we just prefer what the white wine does in the dish. This recipe also has a few subtle twists that make it stand out. Veal shanks are always preferred, but beef shanks work as well. Serve this with risotto, polenta, potato puree or pasta.

Preheat your oven to 350°F (177°C).

Heat the oil in a large Dutch oven that you can cook your shanks inside—depending on the diameter of the shanks, 5 to 9–quart (4.7 to 8.5–L) Dutch ovens should fit everything. Season the shanks with the salt and pepper and sear over medium-high to high heat until a good browning occurs on both sides. This will take about 3 minutes per side. Remove the shanks to a plate and set aside.

Turn the heat down to medium and add the celery, carrot and onion, stirring often with a wooden spoon. The goal here is to soften the vegetables and get a little bit of color on them. This should take about 5 minutes. Add the garlic and stir for about 1 more minute, until fragrant. Add about ¼ cup (59 ml) of the wine and the tomato paste, scraping the bottom of the Dutch oven to deglaze. Add the rest of the bottle of wine and the beef stock and continue to cook over medium heat.

Make your sachet by simply adding all of the ingredients for the herb sachet to a cheesecloth, then tie it securely with kitchen twine. Add the sachet and the shanks to the Dutch oven. The liquid should not cover the shanks completely.

Cover the Dutch oven and place it in your preheated oven for 90 minutes. Check several times to make sure the liquid doesn't evaporate too much. If your liquid nearly evaporates, add more beef stock, if necessary, to keep the level of the liquid covering the shanks at least halfway. After the first 45 minutes, turn your shanks over in the pot and continue to cook. After 90 minutes have elapsed, stir in the cream and balsamic vinegar. Return to the oven and cook for another 15 to 30 minutes, until very tender.

To make the gremolata, simply add the gremolata ingredients together and let sit for at least 10 minutes prior to serving.

When serving the shanks, serve the meat on top of your pasta, risotto or other starch. Spoon some sauce over the meat and add a small amount of gremolata on top.

Serves: 4–6

3 tbsp (44 ml) olive oil, for searing

4 (16-oz [454-g]) veal shanks

2 tsp (12 g) kosher salt

½ tsp black pepper

½ cup (85 g) small-diced celery

½ cup (85 g) small-diced carrot

1¼ cups (175 g) small-diced onion

2 cloves garlic, minced

1 (25-oz [750-ml]) bottle dry white wine, divided

3 tbsp (42 g) tomato paste

1 cup (237 ml) beef or veal stock

3 tbsp (44 ml) cream

2 tsp (10 ml) balsamic vinegar

Herb Sachet
4 sprigs thyme

1 sprig rosemary

3 bay leaves

8 parsley stems

1 star anise

Gremolata
4 tbsp (15 g) finely chopped parsley

Zest of 1 lemon

Juice of 1 lemon

2 cloves garlic, minced

Pinch of salt and pepper

⅛ tsp crushed red pepper flakes

STARTERS, SOUPS, FINGER FOODS AND MORE

Great Beginnings to Any Meal—and Sometimes a Meal on Their Own!

On special occasions at my grandparents' house, we always had multicourse meals that included appetizers, small plates, soups and other delicious things. I still don't know how my grandparents fit the number of people in their house that they did, but it happened. And everything revolved around food, all day long!

I'm sure many people have memories just like this, but for instance, at Thanksgiving a starter may have been a hearty Italian wedding soup, followed by a massive spread of pasta with sauce and an abundance of meats, like chicken, pork, meatballs and sausages. I'm sure there were salads around, but that was of little interest to a ten-year-old boy! After all of this

was served, the traditional American Thanksgiving feast began, which included all the Thanksgiving sides as well. Just when we thought we couldn't eat anymore, Grandma brought out the desserts! Many of these desserts were traditionally American and some were very Italian, but all were delicious if you had room and if you were still awake.

Some of the things in this chapter are delicious items that Angela and I created based on inspiration from foods we had while traveling in Italy. We may have liberally modified them, but that is our progressive attitude toward cuisine. A few items, like Pasta e Fagioli (page 113) and Italian Wedding Soup (page 102), were staples in my family, and we developed our own versions of these traditions to carry on in our family.

Italian Wedding Soup

This is one of the most interesting and important dishes in my family. My family has managed to drive off into different directions regarding how exactly to make it, and every family member claims that their version is the original. My aunt Jean and cousin Lisa make a very hearty version with beef stock that is a meal in itself! Despite the differences between our recipes, my grandpa insisted on one thing every time: The meatballs MUST be small. In fact, my mom tells me that, without fail, Grandpa would let her know that her meatballs were always too large! Our beloved Italian language instructor, Paola, also shared many Italian traditions with us, including her family's version of this soup. We incorporated some of the ingredients her family uses into our version of Italian Wedding Soup here as well, and we feel this delicious version will carry on in our own family for a long time!

Preheat the oven to 375°F (191°C) and line a baking sheet with parchment paper.

Mix the meatball ingredients until thoroughly combined in a large bowl. Make very small meatballs, about the size of your fingernail, or just under ½" (1.3 cm) in diameter. Place on the parchment-lined baking sheet. Bake for 7 to 8 minutes to cook through and get a small amount of browning. Set aside.

For the soup base, begin by bringing a pot of salted water large enough to hold the escarole to a boil. Add the rinsed escarole to the boiling water for 2 minutes. Remove the escarole and thoroughly drain by squeezing it with either paper towels, a cheesecloth or a tea towel to remove the water before chopping. Chop and set aside.

In another large pot, add your cooked meatballs, chicken stock, shredded chicken, chopped escarole, carrot, pepper and salt. Bring to a boil and then gently simmer for 30 minutes. After 30 minutes, mix the Romano cheese with the egg in a small bowl with a fork. Once thoroughly mixed, stir into the simmering soup and stir in thoroughly.

Serves: 10–12

Meatballs

½ lb (227 g) ground chuck

½ lb (227 g) ground veal

1 large egg

1½ tsp (8 g) kosher salt

¼ cup (25 g) bread crumbs (panko or regular, unseasoned)

¼ cup (18 g) finely grated Parmesan cheese

¼ tsp oregano

¼ tsp black pepper

¼ tsp dried thyme

¼ tsp dried parsley

¼ tsp onion powder

¼ tsp garlic powder

Soup Base

1 bunch escarole (see Notes)

10⅔ cups (5 L) chicken stock

1 lb (454 g) cooked chicken meat, shredded and cut into small pieces

1 medium (3-oz [85-g]) carrot, peeled and sliced

½ tsp black pepper

1 tbsp (18 g) kosher salt

¼ cup (18 g) Romano cheese, finely grated

1 large egg

Prepare your garnish by cutting the mozzarella into ¾-inch (2-cm) cubes, then set them aside in the fridge until the soup is ready to serve.

Take your Italian bread and cube it without the crust, creating about ¾-inch (2-cm) cubes. Heat the olive oil in a shallow skillet over medium-high heat and add the bread. Shallow fry the bread, turning once you achieve a light brown crust on each side. This only takes a few minutes, as you are just trying to crisp the bread and add some flavor. Sprinkle with the salt, then remove to a paper towel to drain and dry and set aside to serve with the soup.

The soup can be served in bowls and garnished with a few cubes of mozzarella and fried bread, with Parmesan cheese on the table for your guests to add as desired.

*See photo on page 100.

Notes

The meatballs can be made in advance and frozen, if desired. They do take some patience and time, but it is worth it.

Use spinach if you cannot find escarole.

If you keep Parmesan rinds, you can add one to the broth for a while to add flavor, and then remove it before serving.

Garnish

8 oz (226 g) fresh mozzarella

½ loaf Italian bread

2 tbsp (30 ml) olive oil

½ tsp kosher salt

¼ cup (25 g) finely grated Parmesan cheese

Eggplant Napoleon with Pumpkin Seed Arugula Pesto and Goat Cheese

In cooking, the name Napoleon refers to food that is stacked or layered creating a tower. This results in both a beautiful presentation and a combination of textures and flavors in each bite.

Our version of an eggplant Napoleon combines Parmesan-breaded eggplant slices with layers of roasted cherry tomatoes, our Arugula and Basil Pesto with Pumpkin Seeds (page 153) and goat cheese for an appetizer that is sure to impress.

Preheat the oven to 375°F (191°C).

Place the cherry tomatoes on a baking sheet, drizzle with the olive oil and roll the tomatoes around to coat.

Poke the eggplant slices with a toothpick several times, then sprinkle with the salt and pepper and place on a wire rack over a baking sheet to roast. Cook the tomatoes and eggplant for 15 to 17 minutes, then remove them from the oven and allow them to cool briefly. Transfer the tomatoes to a bowl, gently smash them with a fork and set aside.

Mix together the panko and Parmesan and spread on a plate. Put the flour on a plate next to your bowl of egg and water mixture. Coat each slice of eggplant first in the flour, then in the egg and lastly in the panko.

In a large nonstick skillet, add enough grapeseed oil to cover the bottom completely—this should be about ¼ cup (59 ml) total, but use slightly more or less, depending on the size of your skillet to have a shallow, even layer of oil. Heat over medium heat, then add your breaded eggplant slices. Cook until the bread crumbs have browned, then flip and repeat, 1 to 2 minutes per side. Remove the eggplant to a cooling rack to allow excess oil to drip off for about a minute.

To assemble your Napoleon, place a small amount of arugula leaves on a plate. Directly on top of the arugula, place one eggplant slice. Gently spread some goat cheese on top, followed by some pesto and then some cherry tomatoes. Add another slice of eggplant, then top with a little more goat cheese and cherry tomatoes. Drizzle with balsamic vinegar and high-quality extra virgin olive oil.

Note
Since eggplants are not symmetrical, you may end up with some Napoleons with a small diameter and some with a larger diameter. This recipe will make 4 to 6 Napoleons that vary in size.

Serves: 4–6

1 pint (300 g) cherry tomatoes

Olive oil, for drizzling

1–2 (21–25-oz [600–710-g]) eggplants, sliced into ½" (1.3-cm) rounds

1 tsp kosher salt

1 tsp black pepper

½ cup (43 g) panko bread crumbs

½ cup (50 g) grated Parmesan cheese

½ cup (63 g) all-purpose flour

2 large eggs whisked with 2 tbsp (30 ml) water

¼ cup (59 ml) grapeseed oil, plus more as needed

Large handful arugula tossed in olive oil, for plating

4 oz (113 g) fresh goat cheese

¼ cup (92 g) Arugula and Basil Pesto with Pumpkin Seeds (page 153)

High-quality balsamic vinegar and extra virgin olive oil, for drizzling

Marinated Tomato and Mozzarella Salad

The caprese salad is so classic and beloved, but derivations from it can be amazing. We keep the spine of the classic here, but the simple changes really bring a new flavor to the table. This is another time to bring out a very flavorful and high-quality Italian extra virgin olive oil.

Serves: 4

Place the cut tomatoes, pepper, red wine vinegar and sherry vinegar in a medium bowl, and marinate at room temperature for an hour, stirring gently once to marinate all of the tomatoes.

Add the mozzarella, gently stir and let it sit for 5 minutes. Strain the excess liquid from the bowl and taste for seasoning. Add salt, if necessary. Add the basil and gently mix.

Transfer the salad to a serving bowl and drizzle to taste with your favorite finishing extra virgin olive oil.

12 oz (340 g) cherry tomatoes, cut in half across the equator

½ tsp black pepper

2 tbsp (30 ml) red wine vinegar

2 tbsp (30 ml) sherry vinegar

8 oz (226 g) ciliegine mozzarella, cut in half

Salt, to taste

6–8 basil leaves, rough chopped

Extra virgin olive oil, for drizzling

White Wine and Butter Mushroom Crostini

We love mushrooms and make some version of them almost weekly. When we can find fresh varieties from farmers' markets nearby, we make them even more often. But this recipe adds a tremendous amount of flavor to mushrooms, so you'll be happy even if you use a relatively bland variety of white store-bought mushrooms.

Serves: 4

Preheat oven to 400°F (225°C).

Melt the butter in a medium pan over medium heat. Once the butter has melted, add the mushrooms and toss to combine. Cook for 2 minutes, then add the pepper and oregano and stir to combine. Cook for 1 more minute, or until the mushrooms begin to brown, then add the wine. Scrape the bottom of the pan with a wooden spoon to dislodge any browned bits, called fond, which will provide additional flavor to the dish. Once the liquid is almost completely absorbed, add the salt and parsley and reduce the heat to low. Stir to incorporate. Continue to cook until the wine is completely reduced and absorbed. This will take about 10 minutes.

While your mushrooms cook, place the bread slices on a baking sheet and brush them with the Garlic-Infused Olive Oil. Place in the oven and toast for 7 minutes, or until just starting to brown.

Top the crostini with the mushrooms and shaved Parmesan and sprinkle with parsley to serve.

Note

If you want to make this recipe without the Garlic-Infused Olive Oil, brush the bread with olive oil and toast. After the bread has toasted, rub a clove of garlic that has been cut in half on each piece, then add the mushrooms.

Mushrooms

4 tbsp (56 g) unsalted butter

8 oz (226 g) cremini mushrooms, cleaned and sliced

½ tsp black pepper

1 tsp oregano leaves (2–4 sprigs)

1 cup (237 ml) dry white wine

¾ tsp kosher salt

1 tbsp (5 g) finely chopped parsley

1 baguette, cut into ½" (1.3-cm) slices

2 tbsp (30 ml) Garlic-Infused Olive Oil (page 161; see Note)

Garnish

Shaved Parmesan cheese

Chopped parsley

White Bean and Red Pepper Dip with Garlic Toast

This simple but flavorful dip can be served with anything from vegetables to crackers or, my favorite, garlic toasted Italian bread. Cannellini beans are the basis for this dish and they are fabulous. The canned variety works perfectly in this flavorful dip, so that is the basis of the recipe. However, if you use dried beans, soak them overnight until tender before cooking for best results.

Preheat the oven to 400°F (225°C).

To make the peppers, heat a small skillet over medium heat and add the olive oil. Add the bell pepper and sauté for 3 to 5 minutes, until soft. Add a pinch of salt and pepper and a few drops of lemon juice, stir and remove from the heat. Remove to a small bowl and set aside.

For the garlic toasts, place the bread slices on a baking sheet and brush them with the Garlic-Infused Olive Oil. Place your baking sheet in the oven and toast for 7 minutes while you finish the dip.

For the beans, heat a large skillet over medium heat and add the olive oil. When it is hot, add the beans and garlic to the pan. Cook for about 2 minutes to evaporate some moisture from the beans. Add the salt and pepper and cook for another minute. Add the wine, oregano, thyme and rosemary and cook until the wine has evaporated some and the alcohol smell has gone, about 1 minute. Remove the pan from the heat and transfer the mixture to a bowl.

Mix the bell peppers and parsley with the beans, drizzle with good extra virgin olive oil and serve with the garlic toasts.

Notes
The beans will be quite soft after cooking. We like to mix and mash them up with a spatula, but without trying to create a "puree" type of dip. Our version will have some beans that aren't completely processed, but you can certainly use a mixer to further smooth out the beans.

If you want to make this recipe without the Garlic-Infused Olive Oil, brush the bread with olive oil and toast. After the bread has toasted rub a clove of garlic that has been cut in half on each piece.

Serves: 4–6

Peppers
1½ tbsp (22 ml) olive oil

½ cup (85 g) small-diced red bell pepper

Pinch of kosher salt and black pepper

A few drops of lemon juice

Garlic Toasts
1 baguette, cut into ½" (1.3-cm) slices

2 tbsp (30 ml) Garlic-Infused Olive Oil (page 161; see Note)

Beans
2 tbsp (30 ml) olive oil

2 cups (350 g) canned cannellini beans, drained and rinsed

3–5 cloves Garlic Confit (page 161)

1 tsp kosher salt

¼ tsp black pepper

¼ cup (59 ml) dry white wine

2 tsp (2 g) chopped fresh oregano

1 tsp chopped fresh thyme

½ tsp chopped fresh rosemary

1 tbsp (4 g) chopped parsley

Extra virgin olive oil, for drizzling

Pasta e Fagioli

As my dad says, this recipe was "etched in stone" for Wednesday night supper when he was growing up. As the name indicates, it is just pasta and beans. Of course, there are more ingredients than that, but its foundation is as a peasant dish made with readily available and inexpensive ingredients. It is often a meatless dish, but that was never the case in our family. It is usually a soup or stew, but that is dependent on the region, town and even the family making it! This is so much more than just a peasant soup—I mean, Dean Martin sang about it in "That's Amore!" It is not only a traditional Italian dish, but also one that immigrated to the United States with popularity, and that was true for me growing up. I have taken the liberty to make this even better with a few twists that spruce this up to a dish that's perfect for a cold winter day when you want something warm and comforting.

Heat a Dutch oven or large pot over medium heat. Add the olive oil and pancetta and cook for 5 to 6 minutes or until the pancetta renders and browns slightly. Add 1 teaspoon of kosher salt, black pepper, red pepper flakes and ground beef. Cook until the beef is nearly browned, about 5 minutes, then add the onion and celery. Continue cooking for about 10 minutes, or until the onion is at least translucent and at most, slightly browning. Add the tomato paste and stir until incorporated, cooking for another minute.

Drain your soaked beans from the soaking liquid and discard that water. Add the beef stock, water and marsala to the pot with the beef and bring to a boil. Once boiling, add the beans and return to a simmer. Reduce the heat to low, cover and simmer for 1 hour.

After 1 hour of simmering, add the pasta, additional 2 tablespoons (36 g) of kosher salt, balsamic vinegar and oregano. Gently simmer for an additional 20 minutes uncovered. The pasta should be done and the consistency should be stew-like.

Serve with chopped fresh basil, freshly grated Parmesan and, if desired, additional red pepper flakes.

Note

Alternatively, you can use one 15-ounce (425-g) can of partially drained cannellini beans instead of dried.

Serves: 8

1 tbsp (15 ml) olive oil

¼ lb (113 g) pancetta, finely diced

2 tbsp plus 1 tsp (42 g) kosher salt, divided

Pinch of black pepper

1 tsp crushed red pepper flakes, plus more if desired

1 lb (454 g) ground beef

1 medium (4-oz [113-g]) onion, small dice

1 (1-oz [30-g]) rib celery, thinly sliced

4 tbsp (56 g) tomato paste

1 cup (200 g) dry cannellini beans, soaked overnight (at least 12 hours) in water (see Note)

1 cup (237 ml) beef stock

3 cups (710 ml) water

2 tbsp (30 ml) marsala

1 cup (135 g) dry pasta (small shells or small elbows)

2 tbsp (30 ml) balsamic vinegar

1 tsp chopped fresh oregano

1 tbsp (4 g) chopped fresh basil

Freshly grated Parmesan cheese, to taste

Ricotta "Meatballs" with Quick Tomato Sauce

If you have a vegetarian in the family, or if you love ricotta as much as we do, these are a perfect option. We serve these alone with the sauce as an appetizer or over pasta as a main course. We also enjoy combining these with our regular meatballs from the Spaghetti and Meatballs recipe (page 45) for a combination of ricotta and regular meatballs in one dish. The ricotta "Meatballs" can be served with Grandma's Sunday Sauce (page 145) or Marinara Sauce (page 149) if you already have a batch of those sauces prepared, but we love to make these with this quick tomato sauce in a pinch. Serve with some fresh Italian bread.

Mix all the ingredients for the Ricotta "Meatballs" thoroughly with your hands and roll into balls about 1 inch (2.5 cm) in diameter. Place the balls in the refrigerator for 20 minutes to rest and come together.

At this time, you can make your sauce. Add all the ingredients to a bowl, except for the garlic oil, and mix well with a spatula. Heat a large saucepan that can hold the "meatballs" and sauce over medium heat. Put the garlic oil in the saucepan, if you have it. Otherwise, put the oil in, add the minced garlic and cook for about 30 seconds until fragrant. Immediately add the tomato mixture and bring to a simmer. Simmer, uncovered, for 10 minutes.

Add the ricotta balls to the simmering sauce and cook for 20 to 30 minutes, covered.

Remove from the heat and serve with fresh bread or pasta.

Notes
If you don't have panko on hand, you can also use any other crunchy variety of bread crumbs.

If you don't have any Garlic-Infused Olive Oil, you can use 1 clove of garlic that has been minced or pressed plus 2 tablespoons (30 ml) of olive oil.

Serves: 8–10

Ricotta "Meatballs"
1 lb (454 g) ricotta, drained for 2 hours in a strainer to remove excess moisture

2 cups (200 g) panko bread crumbs (see Note)

1 clove garlic, minced

¾ cup (80 g) Pecorino Romano cheese, grated

¾ cup (80 g) grated Parmesan cheese

2 large eggs

1 tbsp (3 g) finely chopped basil

1 tsp finely chopped oregano

2 tsp (2 g) finely chopped parsley

¼ tsp crushed red pepper flakes

¼ tsp lemon zest

Small pinch of nutmeg

Pinch of kosher salt

Pinch of white pepper

Quick Tomato Sauce
2 (28-oz [794-g]) cans diced tomatoes, with juice

2 tbsp (3 g) dried basil

2 tbsp (3 g) dried oregano

1 tsp crushed red pepper flakes

1 tsp sugar

1 tsp kosher salt

2 tbsp (30 ml) Garlic-Infused Olive Oil (page 161; see Note)

Stuffed Tomatoes

Ironically, I would only eat tomatoes that were cooked as a kid. I still think tomatoes that have been cooked for just one minute are better than raw ones, but now I love and appreciate this ingredient as much as any fruit or vegetable. This version is a spectacular side dish or appetizer that seems so elevated, but is just a basic pairing of flavors. This can be served with almost anything, and it is best when the tomatoes are as fresh as possible.

Preheat your oven to 375°F (191°C). Line a baking sheet with parchment paper.

Start by preparing the tomatoes for stuffing. From the top of the tomato, use a sharp paring knife to cut a small hole and hollow out each tomato. Using a small spoon, scoop out most of the seeds and pulp. Leave as much of the outer flesh of the tomato as possible for taste and to keep it together. Place your tomatoes on the parchment-lined baking sheet.

For the filling, finely chop the basil and parsley and add them to a bowl. Add the bread crumbs, olive oil, salt and red pepper flakes to the bowl and combine thoroughly. Gently stuff the tomatoes with the filling without packing it into the tomatoes. Divide the Parmesan over the top of each tomato. Bake the tomatoes in your oven for 8 to 10 minutes, or until the tops are golden brown.

Remove to let cool for a few minutes and then serve.

Serves: 6–8

10 Campari tomatoes, slightly larger than golf ball size

⅔ cup (40 g) Italian sweet basil

⅓ cup (20 g) Italian flat-leaf parsley

½ cup (42 g) panko bread crumbs

1 tbsp (15 ml) olive oil

¼ tsp kosher salt

½ tsp crushed red pepper flakes

2 tbsp (13 g) grated Parmesan cheese

THE SWEET LIFE

Desserts and Libations

And now we get to the sweet life. I'm just going to start off by saying that I own an Italian gelato maker, and it was one of the best purchases I ever made. I know that's not going to resonate with the majority of people who read this, but it is a heavily used appliance in my world, and I haven't bought ice cream for many years. If you're on the fence about owning one, just do it . . . it's worth the investment.

Angela and I both have a moderate sweet tooth—it's not overboard, but if you tell her that you make a good tiramisù, she will hound you until you prove it! I'm the same way with gelato, if you haven't figured that out, but what I really appreciate is incorporating flavors in the perfect way. It isn't easy to make lavender an effective dessert component. And it's even more difficult to make it memorable. Combining booze with fruit is done all over the world, but to do it in a way that makes you literally shake your head and say: "Wow!" at the concoction is what we're after.

Homemade Gelato

We have been making gelato for years and have included a staple vanilla bean base recipe here that can be modified in so many ways, as well as a few favorites that are a bit off the beaten path. These are packed with flavor, and I find that I never need a large amount of gelato to satisfy that inevitable craving. Note that our gelato maker can handle about 2½ cups (591 ml) of product base, so you can adjust your recipes accordingly with these ratios depending on your machine.

Creamy Vanilla Bean Gelato

This is a baseline recipe that can be changed or added to depending on your own taste. This can certainly be made with vanilla extract or (even better) vanilla bean paste if you do not want to use a whole bean.

Serves: 8

1 cup (237 ml) heavy cream

1 cup (237 ml) whole milk

1 cup (200 g) sugar, divided

Pinch of salt

1 vanilla bean

5 large egg yolks

Combine the cream, milk, ¼ cup (50 g) of sugar and salt in a medium bowl. Split the vanilla bean in half lengthwise and scrape the pulp into the milk mixture, then add the pod in as well. Whisk to combine. Set aside.

In a separate bowl, combine the egg yolks and ¾ cup (150 g) of sugar and whisk until light and fluffy. Pour about ½ cup (118 ml) of the milk mixture into the egg yolk and sugar mixture and whisk until incorporated. Then add the remaining milk mixture and stir to incorporate completely.

Place the contents into your ice cream or gelato machine and mix per your machine's instructions until thickened and creamy. Our gelato machine takes about 30 minutes to churn this flavor.

Once your gelato is done, move it to a freezer-safe container and freeze overnight for best results.

Hazelnut Chocolate Nutella® Gelato

Nutella seems to be in every Italian's DNA, and this nearly 60-year-old product is one of my favorites! Adding some hazelnuts for texture and hazelnut liqueur for extra goodness always gets my mouth watering.

Serves: 8

About 35 minutes before starting this recipe, line a baking sheet with parchment paper and use 4 tablespoons (59 ml) of the Nutella to make about 20 small pea- to marble-sized dollops on the parchment paper. Place in the freezer for 30 minutes, or until ready to use.

Add the hazelnuts to a dry skillet over medium heat and toast for 3 to 5 minutes, or until lightly browned and fragrant. Remove from the heat and allow to cool, then roughly chop. Set aside.

To make the gelato base, combine the cream, milk, ¼ cup (50 g) of sugar, salt, hazelnut liqueur and 2 tablespoons (30 ml) of Nutella in a medium bowl. Split the half of a vanilla bean and scrape the pulp into the milk mixture, then add the pod in as well. Whisk to combine. Set aside.

In a separate bowl, combine the egg yolks and ¾ cup (150 g) of sugar and whisk until light and fluffy. Pour about ½ cup (118 ml) of the milk mixture into the egg and sugar mixture and whisk until incorporated. Then add the remaining milk mixture to the egg and sugar mixture and stir to incorporate completely.

Place the contents into your ice cream or gelato machine and mix per your machine's instructions until thickened and creamy. Our gelato machine takes about 30 minutes to churn this flavor.

Once thickened, add the chopped toasted hazelnuts and frozen Nutella dollops and allow the mixture to churn a few more times to incorporate.

Once done, remove to a freezer-safe container and freeze overnight for best results.

6 tbsp (89 ml) Nutella, divided

⅓ cup (45 g) hazelnuts

1 cup (237 ml) heavy cream

1 cup (237 ml) whole milk

1 cup (200 g) sugar, divided

Pinch of salt

1 tbsp (15 ml) hazelnut liqueur

½ vanilla bean

5 large egg yolks

Lemon Lavender Gelato

I will get a lemon gelato at least once (usually more) every time I visit Italy. I love to see the differences between each gelateria and how different regions of the country each have their own spin on such a classic flavor. Well, this is how we do it, and the very faint lavender scent really works with lemon!

Combine the cream, milk, lemon zest, ¼ cup (50 g) of sugar, salt and lavender in a saucepan. Split the half of a vanilla bean and scrape the pulp into the milk mixture, then add the pod in as well. Heat over medium heat and bring it to a gentle simmer, stirring constantly, for about 1 minute. Remove from the heat and let the mixture steep for 2 minutes, then strain through a fine sieve into a medium bowl. Set aside.

In a separate bowl, combine the egg yolks and ¾ cup (150 g) of sugar and whisk until light and fluffy. Pour a tiny bit, about ¼ cup (59 ml) of the milk mixture into the egg yolk and sugar mixture and whisk until incorporated. Continue pouring a small amount of milk into the egg yolk and sugar mixture at a time and incorporating until half the mixture has been added. Then add the remaining milk mixture and stir to incorporate completely. Add the lemon juice and stir.

Place the contents into your ice cream or gelato machine and mix per your machine's instructions, until thickened and creamy. Our gelato machine takes 40 to 50 minutes to churn this flavor since it starts out warm.

Once done, remove to a freezer-safe container and freeze overnight for best results.

Serves: 8

1¼ cups (296 ml) heavy cream

1¼ cups (296 ml) whole milk

Zest of 2 lemons

1 cup (200 g) sugar, divided

Pinch of salt

¼ tsp lavender

½ vanilla bean

4 large egg yolks

¼ cup (59 ml) lemon juice

Balsamic Basil Gelato with Strawberry Maceration

Feeling a bit funky? This is for you. I'm not sure how to explain this, but I have an absolute fascination with balsamic vinegar, and these flavors in a creamy gelato are truly intriguing. Just try it—we promise you will be at a minimum impressed and possibly addicted to this unique concoction. The strawberry maceration goes wonderfully with this gelato, but it can be eaten with whipped cream, oatmeal or any number of things.

Combine the cream, milk, basil leaves, ¼ cup (50 g) of sugar and salt in a saucepan over medium heat. Bring it to a gentle simmer, then reduce the heat to low. Whisk frequently for 1 to 2 minutes while it simmers, then remove from the heat and let the mixture sit for a few minutes. This gets the right amount of flavor out of the basil. Strain through a fine sieve into a medium bowl to remove and discard the basil leaves. Set aside.

In a separate bowl, combine the egg yolks and ¾ cup (150 g) of sugar and whisk or use a hand mixer, until light yellow and fluffy. Add the balsamic vinegar and whisk to thoroughly incorporate. Pour a small amount, about ¼ cup (59 ml), of the milk mixture into the egg yolk and sugar mixture and whisk until incorporated. Continue pouring small amounts of the milk mixture into the egg yolk and sugar mixture at a time and incorporating until half the mixture has been added. Then, add the remaining milk mixture and stir to incorporate it completely.

Place the contents into your ice cream or gelato machine and mix per your machine's instructions, until thickened and creamy. Our gelato machine takes 40 to 50 minutes to churn this flavor since it starts out warm.

Once done, remove to a freezer-safe container and freeze overnight for best results.

While the gelato churns, you can make the strawberry maceration. Simply add all the ingredients to a sealable container, mix very well and refrigerate overnight. Serve a few tablespoons (30 ml) over the top of a serving of this gelato to really make it decadent!

Serves: 8

Gelato

1¼ cups (296 ml) heavy cream

1¼ cups (296 ml) whole milk

10 small–medium basil leaves

1 cup (200 g) sugar, divided

Pinch of salt

4 large egg yolks

1 tbsp (15 ml) balsamic vinegar

Strawberry Maceration

18 oz (510 g) finely chopped strawberries

5 tbsp (63 g) sugar

¼ cup (59 ml) sherry vinegar

¼ cup (59 ml) balsamic vinegar

2 tbsp (30 ml) dark rum

1 tbsp (15 ml) amaretto liqueur

2 tbsp (30 ml) vanilla extract

Hazelnut Tiramisù

I've had a lot of tiramisù in my life, and I am not the least bit apologetic about it. But all of that eating "experience" led me to developing a recipe that I think is the ONE. Sure, you can buy the ladyfingers, but there is something very satisfying when every component of this is homemade. Trust me, if they tasted worse than store-bought, I wouldn't make them, so you know they are worth the little effort they take to make.

Preheat the oven to 400°F (205°C).

Start by making the ladyfingers. Using a mixer, whip the egg whites, adding a tablespoon (8 g) of the sugar at a time in intervals, 4 tablespoons (31 g) total. Whip until stiff peaks form, meaning that the whipped egg whites will stand up straight when you remove the whisk.

In a different bowl, add the remaining ½ cup (62 g) of sugar and egg yolks and whisk vigorously until the yolks are pale yellow and fluffy and the sugar is mostly dissolved. Add the egg white mixture to the egg yolk mixture and very gently fold together.

Sift the flour and baking powder into a third mixing bowl and very gently fold in the combined egg mixture. Add the mixture into a piping bag with a ½-inch (1.3-cm) tip or cut.

Pipe onto a sheet pan lined with parchment or a silicone baking mat such as Silpat®, either using cookie cutters for more uniform ladyfingers or carefully freehand, to create ladyfingers roughly between 3 and 4 inches (7.5 and 10 cm) long. Bake in the oven for 8 to 10 minutes, or until very lightly browned. Let them cool before using.

To make the mascarpone cream, whisk or mix the egg yolks with ⅓ cup (42 g) of the sugar until the yolks are pale yellow, just as you did with the ladyfingers. In a separate bowl, whisk or mix the heavy cream with the other ⅓ cup (42 g) of sugar, until mostly dissolved and you achieve thickened cream with very soft peaks—you can use a mixer if desired. Add the mascarpone and mix until the cream is thickened to a medium-peak whipped cream consistency. Fold in the egg yolk mixture and set aside.

(continued)

Serves: 10–12

Ladyfingers
4 large eggs, yolks and whites separated

¾ cup (150 g) sugar, divided

1 cup (125 g) all-purpose flour

½ tsp baking powder

Mascarpone Cream
4 egg yolks

⅔ cup (134 g) sugar, divided

1 cup (237 ml) heavy cream

8 oz (226 g) mascarpone

Hazelnut Tiramisù (Continued)

Make the soaking liquid by mixing the cooled espresso, dark rum and hazelnut liqueur.

Once the ladyfingers are cooled you can assemble your tiramisù. We prefer to do this in individual-sized dishes, but this recipe can be made in a 9 x 13–inch (23 x 33–cm) baking dish.

First, soak the ladyfingers in the soaking mixture for just a few seconds so that they absorb the liquid. If you leave the ladyfingers in the liquid for too long, they will fall apart and become mush, so soak for 3 to 5 seconds at most. One by one, lay the ladyfingers on the bottom of the dish you are using to make a base. Then add a layer of the cream mixture. Repeat the process with another layer of soaked ladyfingers and top with a second layer of the cream mixture.

Using a sifter or strainer, dust the top with cocoa powder and immediately refrigerate for at least an hour before serving. When ready, shave or grate some dark chocolate over the top of the tiramisù to serve.

Note

One tablespoon (15 ml) of dark rum is a good baseline to start with. Then add 1 to 2 tablespoons (15 to 30 ml) of additional liquor per your taste. Almond, hazelnut, cognac, more rum—you get the idea. This is where you get some flavor that you like best. I found mine, and this is it! Note that if you want to use almond liqueur, you could also choose to add ½ teaspoon of almond extract to the ladyfinger batter and some sprinkled roasted almonds at the end as well.

Soaking Liquid

2 cups (473 ml) espresso, cooled

1 tbsp (15 ml) dark rum (see Note)

2 tbsp (30 ml) hazelnut liqueur

Topping

3 tbsp (23 g) cocoa powder

Dark chocolate, for shaving before serving

Berries and Vanilla Mascarpone Whipped Cream

At first glance, this may seem simple, but a little bit of liqueur ramps up the flavor and adds some adulting to dessert. You can use anything, but it should complement whatever fruits are in the dessert. There are liqueurs made from all of the ones we listed below, but you could also use crème de menthe, honey liqueurs or, if you don't want alcohol in the cream, ⅛ teaspoon of some sort of extract that complements the fruits and cream.

In a mixing bowl, beat the heavy cream until stiff peaks form. Add the mascarpone, confectioners' sugar, vanilla extract and fruit liqueur. Mix on low until the ingredients are just combined. Be careful to not overbeat the cream or it will begin to separate.

Serve over your mixed berries and garnish with a mint leaf, if desired.

Serves: 8–10

1 cup (237 ml) heavy cream

6 oz (170 g) mascarpone

½ cup (64 g) confectioners' sugar

1 tsp vanilla extract

1 tbsp (15 ml) fruit liqueur

4 cups (600 g) mixed berries of choice (raspberries, sliced strawberries, blackberries, blueberries)

Mint leaf, for garnish (optional)

Blood Orange Elderflower Rosé Granita

Granitas are wonderful, icy desserts that are perfect to enjoy any time of the year! We love making this version with a lovely Italian rosé wine when blood oranges are in season, but it can be made with other citrus fruits as well, such as grapefruit, lemon or regular oranges.

Combine the sugar with the water and stir until the sugar dissolves completely. Combine this mixture with the wine, elderflower liqueur and blood orange juice in a 9 x 13–inch (23 x 33–cm) freezer-safe dish or baking sheet.

Place the dish in the freezer uncovered for an hour, then check it to see if the liquid has started crystalizing. Using a fork, scrape the crystalized liquid to create a slush.

Allow it to freeze for 1 more hour and repeat the scraping. If you feel like it needs more time, check it again in another hour. This process doesn't have to be exact, and your granita will still have the desired flaky texture if you leave it longer.

Scrape once more prior to serving.

Note
A shallow, thin-sided dish will freeze quicker and more evenly. We use stainless-steel hotel pans, but use whatever you have available.

Serves: 6

¼ cup (31 g) granulated sugar

½ cup (118 ml) water

2 cups (473 ml) dry rosé wine

1 oz (30 ml) elderflower liqueur

¼ cup (59 ml) blood orange juice, strained

Spiked Affogato

If you've never experienced the simple joy of an affogato, you're missing out. Gelato and espresso are all you need to have a nice indulgent quasi-dessert. But spiking an affogato is our preference when we want to be a bit extra! Hazelnut and almond liqueur are usually our choices, but there are a number of other additions that work—the sky's the limit here! The quality of the espresso and gelato flavors are the most important.

Add your gelato to a glass, then pour the espresso over the top of the gelato followed by the liqueur.

Serves: 1

1–2 scoops (about 4 oz [113 g]) Creamy Vanilla Bean Gelato (page 121)

2 oz (57 ml) espresso

1 oz (30 ml) hazelnut or almond liqueur

Elderflower Aperol Spritz

If you haven't discovered the Italian aperitif called Aperol, you are truly missing out. This is a great alternative to a mimosa but also an excellent summer drink with a very vibrant color. This version is Angela's favorite. It is a slight twist on the classic Aperol Spritz with the addition of elderflower liqueur and the omission of soda water for a slightly sweeter and more floral hint.

Fill a large wine glass with ice. Add equal parts Prosecco and Aperol, add the elderflower liqueur and garnish with a slice of orange and a mint leaf.

Serves: 1

Ice

4 oz (113 ml) Prosecco

4 oz (113 ml) Aperol

1 oz (30 ml) elderflower liqueur

Orange slice, for garnish

Mint leaf, for garnish

Italian Doe Cocktail

I love to experiment with cocktails, and this is a twist on the Italian Buck. I figured, since Angela loved it so much, I would call it the Italian Doe after the female deer. Now, anytime we want to have a nice amaro-based cocktail, we gravitate toward this one. Even if you have a large alcohol collection, these ingredients may not be on hand, but each ingredient is worthy of having a bottle for experimentation.

Stir the Cynar, Luxardo Bitter and lemon juice on ice for 10 to 15 seconds. Add the ginger beer and bitters and stir just a few times to mix. In a lowball glass filled with ice or with a large format ice cube, strain the stirred mixture in. Garnish with a lemon wheel.

Serves: 1

2 oz (57 ml) Cynar

1 oz (30 ml) Luxardo Bitter

¼ oz (7 ml) lemon juice

2 oz (57 ml) ginger beer

A few dashes of ginger bitters

Ice

Lemon wheel, for garnish

THE BASICS

Foundational Recipes for Cooking a Variety of Italian Dishes and Recipes Throughout This Cookbook

These sauces and other items are either on-hand at all times in our house or easy to make on any given day. We use all of these here quite often. Sometimes we will tweak things a bit to achieve different flavor profiles, but the foundation is there.

A great example is Garlic Confit (page 161). Usually I don't mind peeling garlic, but when there are two or more full heads, it can be tedious. But you get two products in one: Garlic-Infused Olive Oil and the delicious, somewhat sweet, soft gems of garlic. We rarely go more than a day without the comfort of knowing it is at our fingertips when cooking.

I hope you try these and love them as much as we do, and if you are the experimental type, they do lend themselves to a bit of tweaking. These are all about taste, not tradition, although the inspiration is obvious at this point.

Grandma's Sunday Sauce

As I mentioned, my dad and his sisters grew up eating a large pasta meal every Sunday without fail. I'm sure there were other fresh ingredients thrown in when in season and grown in Grandpa's garden in their backyard, but I grew up with a version similar to this one. I've made some alterations over the years, most notably NOT adding every leftover meat from the prior week. This version is now a staple in our house. This is a manageable-sized recipe, but I almost always make 2 to 3 times this amount and freeze it in containers. When I know we are having the sauce, I just get the correct size container out and slowly bring it to temperature in a saucepot.

Add all of the ingredients, except the fresh basil, to a large pot. Stir and bring to a boil. Reduce the heat to low and simmer, uncovered, for 2 hours, using a screen on top to prevent splattering. If the sauce thickens too much, you can thin it with some more water.

Once done, stir in the basil and remove from the heat. Use immediately, refrigerate for up to 1 week or store in portions in the freezer for up to 6 months.

Serves: 12

1 (28-oz [794-g]) can whole peeled tomatoes, with juice, mashed into smaller pieces by hand

2 (15-oz [425-g]) cans tomato puree

1 (15-oz [425-g]) can diced tomatoes, with juice

2 (8-oz [226-g]) cans tomato sauce

4 oz (113 g) tomato paste

1 tbsp plus 1 tsp (24 g) kosher salt

1 tsp black pepper

1 tsp crushed red pepper flakes

1 tbsp (2 g) dried oregano

2 tsp (2 g) dried basil

1 tbsp (2 g) dried parsley

1 tsp dried thyme

2 bay leaves

2 tsp (3 g) garlic powder

1 tsp onion powder

3 tbsp (24 g) dried chopped or minced onion

2 tsp (10 g) sugar

⅓ cup (79 ml) red wine

⅓ cup (79 ml) water, plus more as needed

1 tsp balsamic vinegar

2 tbsp (5 g) chopped fresh basil

Sausage Sauce

This sauce was a passion project for over a year for us. We added, subtracted, changed and recorded things for this recipe each time we made it. We were searching for as close as we could get to perfection and it was a fun journey. We finally found what we think is a spectacular sauce that can be used in a variety of ways. The quality of the Italian sausage is important, of course, so use the best you can find!

To prepare the tomatoes for the sauce, place a medium pot of water on the stove and bring it to a boil. While the water comes to a boil, prepare a medium bowl of ice water for the ice bath and set aside.

Cut out the top core and stem of each tomato, then score the bottom by cutting a shallow X that just barely breaks the skin.

Once the water boils, add the tomatoes and cook for 20 to 45 seconds, or until the peels begin to separate from the flesh where the tomatoes are scored. Next, remove the tomatoes from the boiling water and shock them in the ice bath for a few minutes, until cool. The skin of the tomatoes will now easily peel away from the flesh, but use a paring knife if the skin is a bit stubborn.

Finally, cut the peeled tomatoes into quarters and remove the seeds, then chop them finely and set aside.

For the sauce, in a large nonstick skillet or Dutch oven, cook the sausages over medium heat while breaking them up until completely cooked. Once cooked, remove to a plate and set aside.

Next, add the onion to the rendered sausage fat in the skillet and cook for 3 to 5 minutes, or until barely browned on the edges and translucent. If your sausage is too lean and does not render any fat, add olive oil to the skillet with the onion.

Once the onion is translucent, return the cooked sausages to the skillet, add the finely chopped Roma tomatoes, tomato paste, wine, water, basil, oregano, red pepper flakes, pepper and fennel seeds and bring the sauce to a boil. Once boiling, reduce the heat to a simmer and stir often until the consistency has thickened. This will take 45 to 60 minutes. This sauce should not be too thick but not watery either. If your sauce seems too thin, cook for an additional 10 to 15 minutes. On the other hand, if your sauce seems too thick, add a little more water and stir to thin it out until it is your desired consistency. Taste for seasoning and add salt as needed.

Serves: 4

4 Roma tomatoes, about 21 oz (600 g) total

1½ lb (681 g) Italian sausages (hot, sweet or a combination), removed from their casings

1 medium (8–9-oz [225–250-g]) onion, chopped fine

1 tbsp (15 ml) olive oil (optional)

½ cup (120 g) tomato paste

½ cup (118 ml) dry red wine (Chianti or similar)

1 cup (237 ml) water, plus more as needed

½ cup (15 g) rough chopped fresh basil

2 tbsp (4 g) finely chopped fresh oregano

1 tsp crushed red pepper flakes

½ tsp ground black pepper

2 tsp (5 g) fennel seeds

Kosher salt, to taste

Note

We often enjoy this sauce with the Multipurpose Pasta Dough (page 42) cut to any shape as well as with the different variations of gnocchi. In this cookbook, you can find it included in Potato Gnocchi with Sausage Sauce (page 20) and Italian Sausage Lasagna (page 69).

Marinara Sauce

The term "marinara sauce" is widely used, but the sauce itself can often have dramatic differences from recipe to recipe. This is not meant to be anything but a great sauce that features both fresh and canned tomatoes as well as herbs and a tiny bit of heat from chili flakes. It is different enough from the Sunday sauce and adds variety to our sauce lineup.

Add the fresh tomato ingredients to a large Dutch oven or pot. Cook over medium heat, stirring occasionally, for 60 to 75 minutes, until the tomatoes have broken down completely. At this time, or sooner, you should be able to pull the skins of the Roma tomatoes out with kitchen tongs quite easily and discard them.

Add the canned tomato ingredients to the pot and blend with an immersion blender to smooth out the sauce.

Add the spices and herbs ingredients to the sauce and stir. Simmer for 90 minutes, stirring occasionally.

To finish, add the fresh basil and oregano and stir. Remove from the heat and serve. This sauce can easily be portioned and frozen for future use.

Note

You can peel the tomatoes first if you don't want to pull the skins out later. See the Sausage Sauce recipe (page 146) for instructions.

Serves: 12

Fresh Tomato

1 pint (300 g) cherry tomatoes

8 Roma tomatoes, split in half

½ cup (118 ml) water

1 tbsp (18 g) kosher salt

1 cup (20 g) basil leaves, whole

Canned Tomato

2 (15-oz [425-g]) cans diced tomatoes, with juice

2 (28-oz [794-g]) cans whole peeled tomatoes, with juice

1–2 cups (237–473 ml) water

1 (6-oz [170-g]) can tomato paste

1 (8-oz [226-g]) can tomato sauce

Spices and Herbs

3 tbsp (5 g) dried oregano

2 tbsp (18 g) dried chopped onion

2 tbsp (3 g) dried parsley

1 tbsp (8 g) garlic powder

1 tbsp (7 g) dried fennel seed

1 tbsp (2 g) dried thyme

1 tbsp (6 g) crushed red pepper

1 tbsp (15 g) sugar

¼ cup (59 ml) dry red wine

Finishing

½ cup (10 g) chopped fresh basil

¼ cup (5 g) chopped fresh oregano leaves

Roasted Red Pepper Pesto

Roasted red bell peppers have such a great flavor and make this pesto so flavorful. Walnuts are the nut of choice for this pesto, and toasting them really enhances the overall flavor. To change the look of your pesto, depending on what you want, you could also use orange or yellow bell peppers. Neither are quite as sweet as the red variety, but they are very close and will also result in a great pesto.

To roast the bell peppers, we do it one of two ways:

Method 1: Keep each bell pepper whole, place it directly on the burner of your gas stove and blister and blacken it over high heat, turning to blacken the skin as much as possible. This takes several minutes, but you really want to blacken a good portion of the skin. Put the bell pepper in a bowl and cover with plastic wrap—it will steam itself a bit. Once cool enough, remove the bell pepper and peel the skin off. Then cut it open, deseed and chop.

Method 2: Halve or quarter each bell pepper, remove the seeds and stem and lay them skin side up in a heavy pan under the broil setting of your oven. It should be just a couple of inches (5 cm) from the heating element. Once the skin turns black, about 6 to 10 minutes, remove to a bowl and cover, like in Method 1. Once it is cool enough, peel and chop.

Add the chopped walnuts to a dry skillet over medium heat and toast for about 3 minutes, shaking and stirring the pan often until you can smell the intensified nuttiness. Combine them with the chopped bell peppers, basil, salt, pepper, Parmesan, olive oil and vinegar in a food processor for a coarser texture or a blender for a smoother, finer texture and pulse until you have a consistent texture. This pesto can be heated gently and served with pasta, as a spread for bread, as a sauce for pizza or endless options!

Makes: 1½ cups (355 ml)

2 large red bell peppers

½ cup (58 g) chopped walnuts

½ cup (20 g) packed chopped fresh basil

2 tsp (18 g) kosher salt

¼ tsp black pepper

½ cup (50 g) grated Parmesan cheese

4 tbsp (60 ml) extra virgin olive oil

1 tsp white wine vinegar

Arugula and Basil Pesto with Pumpkin Seeds

This is a different take on the classic basil pesto, and we absolutely love this flavor profile. The arugula brings some peppery spiciness, and the toasted pumpkin seeds go especially well. It can be used with pasta or a variety of meats. We also use it in the Eggplant Napoleon (page 105) recipe in this cookbook.

Combine all the ingredients in a food processor for a coarser texture or a blender for a smoother, finer texture and pulse or blend until the desired consistency is reached.

Note
We use the small, plump green "pepitas" for pumpkin seeds, not the larger, flat white ones.

Makes: 2–3 cups (473–710 ml)

1⅓ cups (27 g) packed fresh arugula

1⅓ cups (27 g) packed fresh basil

¼ cup (35 g) pumpkin seeds, toasted (see Note)

3 tbsp (44 ml) lemon juice

4 tbsp (59 ml) extra virgin olive oil

½ cup (50 g) grated Parmesan cheese

2 cloves garlic, minced

1 tsp kosher salt

¼ tsp black pepper

Homemade Ricotta

This can be used instead of store-bought ricotta and is simple and very fresh-tasting. The best quality and freshest milk will make the best ricotta. You can use it in any recipe that calls for ricotta.

Add the milk and salt to a pot and bring to a light boil over medium heat, stirring occasionally so as not to scald the milk. As soon as it begins to boil, remove from the heat and add the vinegar and lemon juice, stirring constantly for 1 to 2 minutes.

Strain the whey through a fine sieve, reserving the ricotta. Using a cheesecloth or the sieve and gravity, allow most of the liquid to drain from the cheese, which should take about 10 minutes. You can also squeeze the cheese in a cheesecloth for a firm texture, depending on how you will be using and serving it. It should maintain some moisture. Store it in a container and refrigerate for up to 1 week.

Makes: 1¼ lb (567 g) ricotta

1 gallon (3.8 L) whole milk

1 tsp kosher salt

¼ cup (59 ml) white wine vinegar

¼ cup (59 ml) fresh lemon juice

Basil Cream Sauce

This is a great cream sauce addition to other sauces as it is both flavorful and decorative. Think of a tomato sauce that you add a tablespoon (15 ml) of cream to at the end, but instead you use this out of a squirt bottle to dress up your dish. This cream reduction of very simple ingredients delivers richness to almost anything. This cream sauce is drizzled onto your dish at the end to enhance the overall flavor and provide a touch of color, like we did in the Cavatelli with Roasted Red Pepper Pesto Sauce, Basil Cream and Burrata recipe (page 41) in this cookbook.

Makes: ¾ cup (177 ml)

1½ qt (1.4 L) water

3 tbsp plus ½ tsp (60 g) kosher salt, divided

1 cup (20 g) fresh basil

1½ cups (355 ml) heavy cream

⅛ tsp white pepper

Add the water to a medium, 2- to 4-quart (1.9- to 3.8-L) saucepan and bring to a boil. In the meantime, have a strainer ready and get a bowl of ice water prepared to shock the basil. When the water boils, add 3 tablespoons (54 g) of the salt and stir. Add the basil for 10 seconds. Strain the water and put the basil leaves into the ice water. After about a minute, the basil will have completely cooled and you can remove the leaves, dry them well with paper towels and roughly chop them.

If you have an immersion blender, add the chopped basil, cream and pepper to a medium saucepan and proceed to the next step. If you do not, add the cream to a blender with the basil only. Blend for just a few seconds to chop up the basil. Be careful not to overblend this or you could start whipping your cream—2 to 3 seconds is all you need. Pour the mixture into a medium saucepan and add the pepper.

Bring the cream mixture to just a boil over medium-high heat, stirring often. Reduce the heat and gently cook the cream over medium-low to medium heat, until reduced by just under half, stirring often. This will take 15 to 20 minutes. Remove the mixture from the heat. Add the remaining ½ teaspoon of salt and stir, then remove to a container or squeeze bottle and put it, uncovered, in an ice bath to rapidly cool the mixture. Once cooled to room temperature, 8 to 10 minutes, you can use it, or cover it and refrigerate.

This is best used at room temperature, and it will liquefy if you heat it up, so when ready to use again, just remove it from the refrigerator in advance. It will be quite thick when refrigerated but should become less thick and creamy at room temperature.

Infused Olive Oils

There are endless ways to flavor olive oils. Any fresh herb or even fruit zests can be used. However, many additions will require you to keep your oil refrigerated, and they will create a shelf life with your oil. We have two examples that make sense to us, since we use them both quite frequently and the flavor is worth it. You don't have to use extra virgin olive oil, but it does keep enough of its flavor to make it a good recommendation.

Crushed Red Pepper Spicy Olive Oil

Combining these ingredients is all you have to do, and it will let you create a spicy addition to recipes and dishes when you want.

Combine the olive oil and red pepper flakes in a sealable bottle or jar and shake vigorously. Shake the jar once a day for 1 week, then use as desired. This can be kept on the counter.

Makes: 1 cup (237 ml)

1 cup (237 ml) extra virgin olive oil

1 tbsp (6 g) crushed red pepper flakes

Rosemary-Infused Olive Oil

Short rosemary sprigs work best in this recipe, depending on the bottle you are storing them in. The fresh rosemary requires this one to be refrigerated, but it will last up to a month.

Fill two medium bowls with water. To one bowl, add the white vinegar. Thoroughly wash the rosemary sprigs under running water. This is important to get all of the dirt, dust and anything else unwanted off of them. Dunk the rosemary into the vinegar water for a few seconds, then into the fresh water for a few seconds. Dry the rosemary thoroughly. In a small saucepan, add the rosemary and olive oil and heat over medium heat for 7 to 9 minutes. It should be hot but not bubbling. Remove the pan from the heat and let it cool. Once cool, put the entire mixture into a sealable bottle or jar. Refrigerate.

Makes: 1 cup (237 ml)

Water

1 tsp white vinegar

3–5 sprigs rosemary

1 cup (237 ml) extra virgin olive oil

Garlic Confit and Garlic-Infused Olive Oil

This versatile and delicious concoction is a must-have for so many things. The garlic will even be spreadable on firm bread, so think about a souped-up garlic bread! The oil will preserve the garlic, so this can be kept on the counter for as long as it lasts—which won't be long!

In a medium saucepan, over low heat, add the garlic and oil. Gently cook until the garlic becomes fragrant. As soon as the edges of the garlic begin to slightly brown, remove from the heat and let cool in the saucepan. This will take 20 to 30 minutes depending on the temperature of your stovetop. You can then store the garlic in the oil in a glass container in your pantry or on the countertop. Use the garlic oil in cooking and use the confit garlic, which will be soft, somewhat sweet and mellow, to spread on toast, in sauces or in other recipes.

Makes: 20 oz (586 ml) of garlic-infused olive oil and about 30 cloves of garlic confit

2 heads garlic, each clove removed and peeled intact

20 oz (568 ml) extra virgin olive oil

Acknowledgments

First and foremost, I would like to thank Angela, my amazing wife and co-author who has been my partner in everything since we met. She is my inspiration at the least and my everything always. Her love of food pushes me to create, please and inspire every single day! I couldn't ask for a better companion to journey through life with. Her photographs of our creations are here to see in this book and bring to life the dishes like they were put right in front of you to enjoy! To my soulmate, ti amo!

We would both like to thank our families, who have encouraged and supported us along the way in so many direct and indirect ways. To Mom and Dad Perlioni, for giving anecdotes and taste testing, as well as always cooking homemade meals as I grew up. To my brother and sister-in-law, Jason and Debbie, for their ongoing, sincere appreciation for our work and their love of food. To my kids, Kate and Joe, for realizing that the kitchen is my happy place, especially when they cook with me, and for tolerating long-delayed dinners from my cooking experiments.

To Mom and Dad Persicke, for supporting Angela's love of photography and for their enthusiasm in our cooking journey, as well as Angela's sister and brother-in-law, Nicole and Joe, for always providing honest feedback and being the most encouraging taste testers. To Aunt Jean, Aunt Carole and my cousins Lisa, Sheri, Corine, Jim and Jann, for thoughts, stories, recipes and food memories from the distant past of our Italian roots.

To the many supporters of Cooking with Wine who turned this hobby and our passion for food into something that is far beyond what we ever thought it would be. We wouldn't be where we are today without our incredible online food and food photography communities on Instagram. In particular, to the talented team members of Food Capture Collective, who show their support for our journey in so many ways every day!

I'd also like to thank my culinary instructors and classmates in Houston for their support and advice, and for allowing me a place to share ideas and learn. Most notably, I'd like to thank Chef Olivier, Chef JR, Chef Pascal and Chef Kirby. Having progressive thoughts about food, especially in a "mother cuisine" such as Italian, can be daunting and even intimidating, and having experienced and talented sounding boards is a tremendous help.

To our Italian language instructor, Paola, for getting us closer to our goal of being fluent Italian speakers. Immersing ourselves in our lessons and then testing recipes afterwards has made this culinary odyssey that much more enjoyable.

I also want to thank Gabriel and Maria Beltran—lifelong friends and business partners who have always been there with genuine encouragement for us.

To Madeline Greenhalgh and the amazing team at Page Street Publishing, for their support, patience and guidance throughout this process. We wouldn't have been able to complete this journey without your incredible expertise and advice.

Finally, to my grandparents, August and Lena Perlioni, for carrying on our Italian traditions and keeping our Italian heritage alive, which ultimately is the main reason I love cooking today. I wish you both were still with us to experience this journey, but your legacy lives on through every dish we create.

About the Authors

Mark Perlioni and Angela Persicke are the food-loving couple who created the blog Cooking with Wine and the @cooking_with_wine Instagram account to share their passion for cooking. Together they create delicious recipes and share drool-worthy images that will make you want to reach into the photo and take a bite! Mark is a business owner and entrepreneur but has had a lifelong passion for cooking. At the end of 2020, he decided to put that passion to practice and completed professional culinary training through the Culinary Institute Lenotre in Houston, Texas. Angela discovered her love for food photography along this cooking journey with Mark while completing her doctorate in psychology, behavior analysis specialization. Mark and Angela's recipes and images have been featured online and offline in publications including Southern Cast Iron, The Purist, feedfeed, Taste of the South and Food Gawker. They currently work with top food and beverage brands for recipe development and food photography.

Index